PADDLES AWAY:
A Psychological Study
Of Physical Punishment
In Schools

By Adah Maurer

PALO ALTO, CALIFORNIA

Published By

R & E Research Associates, Inc.

936 Industrial Avenue
Palo Alto, California 94303

PUBLISHERS

Library of Congress Card Catalog Number

81-51456

I.S.B.N.

0-88247-599-1

PADDLES AWAY!

A Psychological Study of Physical Punishment in Schools

ACKNOWLEDGEMENTS

There are too many people to thank for help in writing this book: Bob Myers who inspired the prologue, Trudy Williams who said, "Cut the polemics," Bix Newhard who approved the medical information, Alan Button who wrote the The Authentic Child; Hal Zuckerman who runs an impossible school with cheerful insouciance and is teaching a whole generation the art of post-violence. My thanks to the 3000 members of END VIOLENCE AGAINST THE NEXT GENERATION, Inc., to the American Psychologist for permission to reprint and to Fred Strassburger who first convinced me that anyone would listen. To Edna Mills of Boone, Michigan who wrote "Lift Holy Hands" and to the First Unitarian Church of Berkeley who let me preach the sermon there one cold January morning in 1973 and who came along to the meeting of the school board to make sure they voted to outlaw corporal punishment. My thanks to Irwin Hyman of Temple University and the National Center for the Study of Corporal Punishment and Alternatives in Schools that he heads. My gratitude to John Poole of the Union Graduate School-West who accepted the original thesis as the P.D.E. for a PhD. To Leona Egeland who authored and carried through to enactment the California law permitting paddles only after parents have put their approval on file in writing in the school office, my deepest admiration. A very special warmth to David Bakan whose Slaughter of the Innocents taught me more about children than did Bettelheim's Love Is Not Enough.

When corporal punishment is finally abolished the credit will go to the activist among the American People who saw a dirty evil and cleaned it up. Among them first credits must go to the American Civil Liberties Union in the persons of Alan Reitman, organizer and Nat Hentoff writer, who took the lead early in the 70's. In Britian it is Peter Newell, Tom Scott and their friends who organized S.T.O.P.P. and took the matter of caning to the European Court of Civil Rights - and won. Or perhaps first credits

V

should go to the cartoonists, Morrie Turner, George Smith, "Funky Winkerbean" and the others who have poked fun at the abusers instead of at the vulnerable.

Parents Anonymous, Jolly K. and all the devoted people who have made this country aware of child abuse and have done something about it. Among those most caught up in its toils are Walter Mondale who sponsored a bill to provide funding for regional child abuse centers, and David Gill, at Brandeis University who pointed out the effect, one upon the other, of parental abuse and legalized institutional abuse of children. All these have contributed to this book.

The two Jims: James Wallerstein whose generosity has made possible the clipping service and the continued publication of <u>The Last ? Resort</u> the newsletter that tries to keep up with the court cases, the changing regulations and to spread the word; Hamish (Jim) Cary, publisher of the <u>Thunderbolt</u>, the kids magazine against paddles. Lastly, thanks to my thousands of students and my own 7 children who by becoming fine people have proved me right.

PROLOGUE

QUIET DIES THE MORNING

They put me in the eighth grade the first time I
opened my mouth. Fortunately my uncle warned me to say
"Sir," at the end of every sentence and at the
beginning of the next, or they might have killed me on
the spot. I was a stranger and they didn't cotton to
much to others. Now I'm even talking like them.

I was only there from the middle of March. My
great-grandfather died and my folks had to go down to
this little town in Kentucky to settle some business.
They thought it would be educational. They always
think that staying out of their way has to be
educational one way or another. Mostly it is. I've
been some neat places and made a lot of friends. But
this three months was something else.

What I learned, mainly, was that I don't want to
go in for anthropology. For field work you have to go
live with some primitive tribe, eat their food and do
like they do. Then you write a book about it. Well
I've done field work and I will write this assignment
about what happened, but that's going to be it. No
more tribes for me. It left me nearly a nervous wreck.
The nightmares are fading, but I still wish I could
have done something to save Robbie.

Most of the paddlings were for talking or cutting
up. It wasn't exactly forbidden; in fact it went on
all the time but if the teacher wasn't in the mood for
it, watch out. The first one I witnessed was the
afternoon of my second day. Mr. B stepped out into the
hall to talk to someone and we all relaxed, but he must
have given some kind of signal because suddenly just
before he opened the door everyone clammed up except
two guys who kept on laughing. They were ordered up to
the front of the room and told, "Assume the position."
They got three blows apiece with all the force a 200

pound man could muster. I can't really explain how I felt. Frightened, yes, but numb and feeling nothing at the same time. They let out an explosive grunt with each blow but otherwise there wasn't a sound. I thought he would never stop and only realized I had been holding my breath when it was all over. I couldn't look at anyone. I was afraid to hang my head for fear of looking guilty. I was paralyzed.

Each teacher had a paddle, most of them about 12" X 5" and half an inch thick. One had his initials drilled in his, "E.Z." and over them was burnt in "not so." Another one had "applied psychology" in red crayon. I doubt if the thought of ever being without their special homemade "teaching tool" ever crossed their minds. They'd feel naked. Robbie told me everyone's got one. When anybody gets married, he said, and have a baby that's the first gift they get. A paddle. He didn't believe me when I said I never heard of such a thing. "Didn't you ever go to school before? How come you spell so good?"

One day the teacher announced that the class had done poorly on a test and each one who failed would be paddled. Again I froze. Not for myself, but for Robbie. He was undersized with a scrawny neck and freckles pocked with poison ivy scars. Tears began running out his nose and he snuffled. His thin body trembled. He was the first to take the beating and he kept on snuffling while the rest of the class took their turns. Less than half were spared.

Robbie said he was used to it. He should have been. He was the most beaten boy, taking it an average of twice a week. He was beaten for throwing a snowball and confessing it although no rules against it had been announced and all the others lied. His worst beating was for trying to be helpful. One afternoon he volunteered to sweep the hall, a dusty trail of soil between the front entrance and the back playground exit. He swept up a sizeable pile and, hoping his teacher would notice, asked him what to do with it. In a jovial mood he suggested that it be swept under the door of Mr. Q's room. Robbie should have known better, but he was trying too hard to curry favor. "Yes, sir," he said.

Mr. Q was strange, really unbalanced, I would say. He spent all day whacking his paddle, the largest one in the school, on the table top, against a tin locker, anywhere at all, just to see people jump. He was vicious and vinegar faced. No one liked him, not the students, not the other teachers. He was as much a

butt of nasty jokes as Robbie was a butt of the paddle.
When he saw the swirls of dust curling up under his
door, he grabbed his paddle and burst out of his door
in a rage. "Get that stuff out of here!" Robbie began
sweeping it down the hall and Mr. Q swatted in time to
the sweeps all the way to the back exit. The hall soon
filled with laughing and hooting boys and teachers who
thought the whole performance awfully funny.

Only once did a student protest. A bigger boy, I
think he was 16 but still in the eighth grade, was
beaten for some trivial offense and he wanted an
apology after his father told him he was a fool for
taking it. He went to the principal and told him what
his father had said. The principal agreed that it was
too much for too little but said "I can't uphold a
student over a teacher, now can I?"

When I heard that something in me died. I was
only 13, but suddenly I was cynical about a system of
authority where status was more important than doing
the right and honorable thing. I began to see
similarities in my world in Massachusetts and in my
father's business and in history and I didn't like it.
These weren't as crude and cruddy as the nasty school I
was a part of for a while, but I can't get it out of my
mind.

I hate that system. I think they ought to be
forced to bring their ways up to date and not make all
those kids spend their school days fighting back tears
and embarrassment. I personally never was hit but I
hurt just the same and I keep on hurting although I
left Kentucky and won't ever go back if I can help it.

CHAPTER ONE

IT HAPPENS

Until the 1970's, swats in school had been a taboo topic. This strange, yet common practice of applying pain as a learning aid was almost never discussed by educational experts. Teachers in training could go through six years of serious study of the educational process and never hear it mentioned, yet find it was the first thing that confronted them when they stepped in front of a class on their own. Most of those who used it routinely in their classrooms or offices shrugged off any discussion secure in the traditional belief that spanking children is just not controversial. For others it was a matter for ribald laughter and triple puns about the board of education.

Most Americans were, or pretended to be, shocked and disbelieving. "I didn't think they did that anymore!" They had read David Copperfield, of course and ancient tales of the schoolhouse on the prairie where lurked the traditional bully who had to be beaten in a fair fight before the new school master was free to win the trust of the crippled kid in the back row and the heart of the village belle. In the enclaves of the fortunate who grew up without having had to run the gauntlet of grim adults, people thought of these tales as sentimental nostalgia of a great-grandparental day, along with rattlesnakes, dry water holes and a multitude of pioneer hazards that were overcome with resiliant heroics. That such an anarchronism as beating children should still exist in these, the last days of the twentieth century, could only be called absurd. The outhouse, body lice and household vermin were, with the hickory stick equally antique, mere memories of a past nastiness that made the good old days a doubtful paradise.

We fooled ourselves. _Time_ magazine captioned a picture from the archives, "As a teaching tool, the hickory stick ranks with such pedagogical fossils as the dunce cap and McGuffy's Reader." _Time_ was not alone in assuming progress but only the name has

1

changed. The hickory stick is now a paddle, a belt or a cane and "swats," "licks," "hacks," or some local euphemism are a commonplace expectation, not only in the dark pockets of cultural lag but for more than three quarters of all American children. Our collective blind spot allowed the hickory stick to be replaced by a wooden weapon, often of fearsome dimension and drilled with welt-raising holes. Paddles flourish in inner cities, in rural prairies, in mountains, in valleys and almost everywhere children go to school.

Kenneth B. Clark, author, educator, President of the American Psychological Association and now member of the Board of Regents for the State of New York, tells with searing honest how he fooled himself:

Like many of my friends and associates I pretended to be shocked and amazed that corporal punishment was taking place in any public school in New York City in the latter part of the twentieth century. But the memory of these casual admissions (by teachers who felt free to beat up the children)...protected by the cloak of anonymity, blocked me from accepting my own pretense of ignorance. For over ten years I knew and had published statements by teachers in the New York City Public Schools that they had inflicted corporal punishment upon children in ghetto schools because "they are accustomed to it and they like it."

...I cannot plead ignorance of the fact that children were victims of physical punishment.... After publishing the verbatim comments of these teachers, I, like many others, remained silent and permitted this evil to persist. With the publication of this new set of charges (in the New York Times) the time for silent acceptance of this disgrace has come to an end.

Dr. Clark also wrote sadly of the "parents (who) sought to justify the use of corporal punishment even as they were denying that it was used."

A Citizen's Commission to investigate the charges of the illegal use of corporal punishment at Junior High 22 was formed and their report confirmed that fact and made recommendations. This first of these was:

Corporal punishment of children - an inheritance from the English common law and traditions under which children were not treated as persons entitled to any rights - must be recognized by all personnel of the public school system as archaic and violative of human dignity

2

and of the rights of students as person. School authorities must, in the words of the Supreme Court, perform their duties "within the limits of the Bill of Rights."

Dr. Clark and the Citizen's Commission had assumed that the Supreme Court would uphold the Eighth Amendment to the Constitution forbidding cruel and unusual punishment. It had not yet been tested. When those decisions were announced in 1975, 1977 and 1980 they were widely misinterpreted. A fuller discussion will be found in Chapter 10 but here it will be enough to note that the Court held parents and teachers responsible for the elimination or the continuation of the custom of using corporal punishment. The 1975 decision held that:

> School officials are free to employ corporal punishment for disciplinary purposes until in the exercise of their own professional judgment or in response to concerted pressure from opposing parents, they decide that its harm outweighs its utility.

Thus if the custom of hitting children in school is to be changed the responsibility has been placed squarely on the shoulders of the American people. An informed public being essential to democratically achieved decisions the conspiracy of silence, whether deliberate or by negligence, needs be ended by a spate of books, broadcasts and debates.

This book is one response. Its purpose is twofold: to prove to the uninformed, the unbelieving and the self-deceived that corporal punishment happens in American schools to a disgraceful degree and to convince its fairminded practitioners that it is unwise, unnecessary, and does irreparable harm to the minds and hearts of each succeeding generation. It is damage we can no longer afford since the modern world of computers and controlled energy takes brains rather than brawn, sophisticated manipulation rather than violence, and creative daring rather than mindless obedience. It there was possibly any rationale for beatings back in the horse and buggy whip days, there is none now that guided transport is pre-programmed and does not respond (except possibly by breaking down) to a gee and a haw and a slash on the rump.

We will consider historical, psychological, medical, sexual, racial, religious and legal aspects. There will be offered a wide range of alternatives. We will advocate discipline of the only kind that is permanent, that is, self discipline acquired from self discipline models and a healthy helping of self esteem. We will advocate diligence due less to duty than to total fascination with facts and feelings by the intellectually curious child. We will advocate respect earned by the adult by his worthiness in the eyes of the child and of the world.

IT DOES HAPPEN HERE

The first modern survey of corporal punishment practices was undertaken in California. Self reports for the school year 1972-73 turned up 46,022 instances of the use of paddle or strap, not counting whatever may have happened in Los Angeles where they could not bring themselves to count. Most of the recipients were younger children. Less than 5 percent of the blows were expended on high school students large enough to be any real threat to the teachers. During that year 535 parents complained that the punishment was too severe, was not deserved or that their child had been seriously injured. Most were satisfied with the explanation or apology or other action, but 63 took the next step of bringing it to the attention of the Board of Education and 7 entered suit for damages. One of these involved an eleven year old boy who had required medical attention for injury to the testes. The principal who had strapped him was contrite and paid $2000 in damage settlement out of court. The school board also agreed that no corporal punishment would be given without expressed parental permission. Five times as many boys were paddled as girls.

A national survey was attempted by the Office of Civil Rights in 1975-76 and although the response was poor and extrapolations necessary, more than a million and a half instances of formal sessions with the paddle were admitted to. The actual figure may have been from 5 to 10 times that, but a pattern did appear. The most corporal punishment was confessed to, or boasted about, in the same section of the country were support for education is the poorest: the Old South, and to a lesser extent, the Sunbelt States of Texas, New Mexico and Oklahoma.

Defenders of the practice, however, continue to insist that it is a rare occurrence, "only one tool among many," and is used "only as a last resort," after all other methods have been tried and failed. But enough cases, treated seriously and humorously, turn up in the back pages of enough local newspapers to make one suspect that just below the surface is a noisesome stench of unreported mayhem that needs to be exhumed, examined and dealt with. A few examples:

In Shelbyville, Tennessee, Cheryl Johnson

4

collected her two-year-old Tony from his first day at
nursery school and found 25 welts on his back when she
prepared him for bed. The school operator said she had
switched him "a time or two" across the shoulders
because he was squatting down with his head between his
legs at the time. She had punished him because he did
not stop crying when his mother left. She told the
judge that in 15 years in the business she had never
received a complaint for her treatment of the children.

Coaches have a lot of fun. One held an open knife
upright under the chest of a nine year old who was
having trouble meeting his quota of push-ups. It was
the newspaper reporter who discovered that the boy had
an improperly healed broken elbow and could not extend
his left arm fully. Another instructor of Health and
Physical Education tied 5 boys to his motorcycle and
dragged them around the parking lot because they had
"wasted his time." He was defended by his superior
because he had painted the scrapes and bruises with
antiseptic before sending them home. In Rapides
Parish, Louisiana, the coach has too few candidates for
the Junior High football team and cannot afford to drop
any for failing grades. Instead, he paddles them. A
round dozen lined up to be whacked for academic "D's"
but one jumped during the beating and went home with
bruises on more than his buttocks. His father
objected. Near Seattle, Washington, the coach followed
the long distance runners in his VW and hopped out
every mile to give the last man a "hacking."
But in Corry, Pennsylvania, the fun is over. At
kickball any player whose ball hit the ceiling took his
lumps and limped home until too many parents objected.
The coach tried to defend himself. "It's just a
ritual, purely for laughs, nothing more than a harmless
diversion." he promised to stop and was forgiven. Yet
the same newspaper also carried the story of the
accusation by the Teacher's Organization that student
violence was not being prosecuted severely enough.
In Cleveland, a seventeen-year-old young woman in
a work/study program was assigned to the office of a
minor city official to do clerical work. Her father
could not understand her reluctance to go to work. She
was lazy, he thought. Finally, she could take it no
longer and described to her father the punishments she
was taking for mistakes. Her employer was in the habit
of tying her up and spanking her. He was charged with
battery and misconduct, but he escaped prosecution.
The girl was a "student" and this was legally
recognized a punishment. It was not abuse or attempted
assault. It was discipline. To be sure, he lost the

5

Where paddles swing

Percent of pupils receiving formal corporal punishment

NATION   3.5

Mass.	0	Calif.	0.7	Ind.	4.3
N.J.	0	Mont.	0.8	Mo.	4.3
R.I.	0	Colo.	0.95	W. Va.	4.5
Hi.	0	Mich.	1.2	S. Car.	5.0
N.H.	0.007	Ak.	1.4	N. Car.	5.2
Maine	0.05	Wash.	1.6	N. Mex.	5.2
Minn.	0.06	Ore.	1.6	Ohio	5.4
N. Dak.	0.06	Penn.	1.65	Ky.	6.7
N.Y.	0.07	Va.	1.7	Ala.	7.0
Wisc.	0.09	Kans.	2.0	Tenn.	8.8
S. Dak.	0.09	Ida.	2.1	Tex.	9.2
Vt.	0.1	Wyo.	2.3	Ark.	10.2
Conn.	0.1	Del.	2.6	Miss.	10.2
Utah	0.13	Ariz.	2.8	Okla.	11.1
Neb.	0.25	La.	2.9	Ga.	11.4
Md.	0.5	Nev.	3.3	Fla.	11.4
Iowa	0.6	Ill.	3.4		

The Office of Civil Rights of the U.S. Department of Health, Education and Welfare, conducted a survey of disciplinary actions taken against school children in the 1975-76 school year. The figures that resulted are carefully labelled estimates and the warning is added that although this is the most reliable data obtainable, they must be interpreted with caution for several reasons:

1. Form 101 asking for enrollment, ethnicity, special education and other facts was sent to all 15,715 school districts, but form 102 which included the question on corporal punishment was sent to a sample of 3,617 (43,738 schools).

2. The question asked was: The number of pupils who received corporal punishment administered by a principal or his designee as a formal disciplinary measure. Thus all punishments by teachers in classrooms or halls, by coaches on the field, by bus drivers, aides or other persons were not counted.

3. Many districts, according to the introduction to the report, submitted incomplete, inaccurate, or inconsistent data. Of all the disciplinary questions (suspensions, expulsions, transfers, etc.) item 17g, corporal punishment, had the highest non-response rate.

The figures here are those reported by each state extrapolated to represent the whole school population of the 1975-76 school year and expressed as a percentage of the total enrollment for the school year 1976-77.

It is obvious that the actual number of incidents of corporal punishment was much higher than this. Some school administrators consider paddling (licks, swats, hacks, pops, or other local euphemisms) to be a trivial necessity, not worthy of federal attention. Some have the grace to be embarrassed by the numbers while others boast of their scores as an indication of toughness, believing it to be a virtue others are afraid to match. These varying attitudes necessarily influence estimates. Sometimes the chore is delegated to a harrassed secretary only peripherally aware of the facts.

Regional differences, however, are probably valid. They match information gathered from newspaper editorials regarding the Supreme Court decision of 1977, from reports of the deliberations and decisions of local school boards, and from the court cases entered by angry parents against schoolmen who have committed atrocities in serious misuse of their authority and have permanently injured children.

1,521,896 KIDS BEATEN AT SCHOOL

next election because of the publicity, but the courts found no fault in his behavior.

A retarded young lady came home with black and blue marks in the shape of a hand on her thighs and back. Her mother protested to the teacher, the principal, the school board, her physician and finally the police. Nowhere could she find anyone who would listen or take her complaints seriously. Tired of her calls, a police officer told her sharply, "Look, lady, it's legal."

The father of a ten-year-old boy sued for $125,000 because his son was paddled without have been given due process rights. The father of another ten-year-old sued for $35,000 accusing the teacher of knocking the boy down and injuring his back so severely that he had to be hospitalized. An $80,000 damage suit was filed in Little Rock for injuries sustained by an eleven-year-old girl who was pounded with a heavy wooden cudgle for failure to complete her homework. An emotionally disturbed boy was thrown down and stomped on by an emotionally disturbed teacher. The child could not explain the size 12 footprints on his white shirt. In Upper Dublin, Pennsylvania the parents did not like the "atmosphere of fear" and said their children were having nightmares. The superintendent ordered the first grade teacher to stop swatting, but she went ring on and was defended at the hearing by the Teachers' Association. In McCormick, South Carolina, Mrs. Jennings may have been too tired to paddle so many. She lined up all those who had not done their homework and had them swatted by all those who had. Twenty students were given one swat each by 89 of their fellow students. The teacher is out on $3000 bail. In East Chicago, little Frankie Lee was hospitalized with stomach injuries; the superintendent said the over use of corporal punishment is under investigation. A child's head was slammed against a concrete wall because, the principal said, he spilled some popcorn.

A refugee from Spartanburg, South Carolina told this story: "There was this one teacher, he was the maths teacher and he ended up in the hospital. He'd whip you even if you didn't bring in your homework. He made this thick strap and tied it to a stick on the end. And all the guys they hated that strap because it really hurt. I sort of think the kids got him and beat him up because of the whippings, but he never did say why they beat him up. After that, he brought a gun to school because, he said, he had to defend himself."

And it is not unheard of that aggressive boys occasionally turn on their tormentors with guns of their own.

7

These few stories represent the tip of an iceberg of brutality and insult that are routine expectations of American school children. The full extent of the problem can only be estimated from the fact that laws in only four states expressly forbid corporal punishment: New Jersey, Massachusetts, Maine, and Hawaii. Maryland attempted to abolish by a school board ruling, but the legislature granted exceptions to the rural counties that requested. Seventeen states specifically provide that physical punishment may be used and some do not allow school boards to forbid. It other states that do not mention the matter, the common law prevails, and the common law, inherited from England, considers the teacher to be acting in loco parentis, (in place of the parent) with the right and duty to chastise as a parent would. Courts in these states acting under medieval English law have ruled that the teacher may not kill the child, nor permanently cripple him, but anything less than that, not matter how severe, is justified.

Local regulations by school boards, and standards set by individual school administrators vary from sadistic to benign. Depending upon the section of the country, the degree of opulence, whether urban or rural, the religious peferences and other factors, children may be at great risk, or hitting a child be unheard of. In Chicago, there was established not only the rule, but what is far stronger, the custom of never laying a hand on a child. From the days of Jane Addams no teacher has carried a paddle and until 1970 no principal wielded a strap. Briefly in the early 70's there was a flurry at the adjustment school but a court case won an out of court agreement to retain the policy forbidding all forms of corporal punishment and to cease turning a deaf ear to infractions. A latter day reformer, Edith Blair, superintendent of District 13 took a leading role in resolving the issue by declaring she would not tolerate the striking of any student. She had gained local fame for restoring peace to a ghetto school without using physical punishment. Any report, she insisted, will be dealt with by strict action including dismissal of any staff member found guilty. During those same years, Dallas, Texas, was earning the label of Corporal Punishment Capital of America. (It has since lost that laurel to Dade County, Florida.)

People who live in protected places sometimes receive a sever culture shock upon settling in a rougher place. Scientists and skilled technicians moving from northeastern states: New Jersey, Massachusetts, New York City, Montgomery County,

8

Maryland, Chicago and University communities generally, into the Sunbelt States to build the newer technologies send their young children to school and go through a cycle of disbelief, indignation, to political action if necessary or to private schools. It may be that the very mobility of Americans will be the factor that will bring more enlightened ways to pockets of cultural lags.

Eliot Wigginton, in his introduction to Foxfire I described a cultural clash in a high school in Georgia:
...I had just finished five years at Cornell. I had an A.B. in English and an M.A. in teaching, and I thought I was a big deal...so I took a job at the 240 pupil Rabun Gap Nacoochee Schools.... Rabun Gap is right in the Appalachians. God's country, as they say here, and I'll go along with that.

About six weeks later I surveyed the wreckage. My lectern (that's the protective device a teacher cowers behind while giving a lecture nobody's listening to) was scorched...set it on fire...Barlow knife...graffiti...nine water pistols...paper airplanes...

The answer was obvious. If I were to finish out the year honorably, it would be necessary to reassert my authority....First offense would be an "X" in the grade book. Second, a paddling. Third, to the principal. Fourth, out of class for two weeks.

It frightens me to think how close I came to making another stupid mistake...more Silas Marner....

The next day I walked into class and said, "How would you like to throw away the text and start a magazine?"

...It is run by high school students who are going on to college knowing that they can be forces for constructive change, knowing that they can act responsibly and effectively rather than being always acted upon.

"To act responsibly as forces for constructive change." Surely this is what we want for all our children. It can be confidently predicted that when we, as did the editor of Foxfire, begin to listen to and to appreciate what the students themselves have to offer, and to recognize that boredom is the root cause of the restlessness that seems to make the paddle a necessity we will begin in reality to build a new America.

To get a better perspective, it may be well to

9

glance at beginnings: The migration of the Puritans from England was also a break with the caning tradition of the English Public Schools. Only 18 years after the Mayflower landed the struggling colony had prospered enough to open a college for the training of clergymen and other learned leaders. Students at Harvard in these early days were the age of high school students now and might have been expected to require a certain amount of discipline. The first headmaster lasted less than a year.

"It is customary for historians of Harvard to pass over the embarrassing debacle concerning Master Eaton as quickly as possible," writes Kathryn Moore in History of Education Quarterly. He was caught beating an usher (junior assistant) with "a walnut log big enough to kill a horse." That and other beating and abusive treatment were intended to bend the scholars to his will. As headmaster, he claimed the right to do with them as he would. There were two questions to be decided at his trial: 1. Shall school masters have absolute power over their students? 2. Shall discipline at Harvard be based on physical force or verbal persuasion? Master Eaton, just as most schoolmen before the courts today, did not deny the punishments; he merely justified them as his right and duty. A modern get-tough-on-youth judge might have acquitted Eaton and praised him for curbing juvenile delinquency. But in seventeenth century Harvard, Eaton was convicted and removed from his position. He ended his life in debtor's prison back home in London. Concluded historian Moore:

> The trial set a precedent concerning Harvard discipline;...the guiding purpose was to bring the student to reason...rather than simply repress or punish his behavior. Clearly if repression or simple punishment were the goal...Eaton, as master, should have been allowed absolute control over the students and permitted to use any means he could to devise to (subdue them). However, if reform were the objective...this involved a consideration not only of the rights and objectives of the master, but also...of the students.

Progress has not been steadily forward. The litany of horrors in nineteenth century schools has been told by the protesters and reformers of those days led in 1848 by Horace Mann who ascribed to the flogging schools the motto, "Fear, Force and Pain." The sorry story was told again by Herbert Falk in 1941 and by Norma Cutts in 1857. Probably each had some small

10

effect as student readers reached positions of authority in educational systems but much of the gain has been wiped out by periodic drives against "permissiveness" that never existed, and juvenile crime that is always labelled a "rising tide."

If some progress has been made, the children in Bloomington, Indiana do not know it. Psychologist Doris Jefferies taught courses there at the University of Indiana to prospective school counselors. She accompanied her first students to their assignments in Bloomington schools and was appalled. As she told it to the 1972 convention of the American Psychological Association:

> At the demonstration school, paddling is so widely accepted that the teacher who generally tries to present the best possible decorum to the outside observer, deliberately includes paddling as part of he master teacher classroom management demonstration...
>
> All day long the paddle swings. Teachers, counselors and administrators walk through the halls carrying their weapons. One child was paddled for singing in the lunch line. The paddle swung against a six-year-old who leaned over to whisper to a friend, "I'm cold," on a blustery Monday morning in winter in a classroom with wide open windows. The teacher pounced, yelled and paddled him for talking. Countless other incidents of equal absurdity were observed every day.
>
> We interviewed the children as they sat outside the principal's office waiting to be punished. The primary age children did not understand the reason for the impending punishment. After they had been paddled they still could not explain the reason for it, only that they were to return to the classroom to "sit down and be quiet." An older child said, "I've got too much pride to let that teacher hit me in front of the class so I got sent to the office."
>
> At the end of the school year, a child had to undergo medical treatment in an attempt to save his left eye that was accidentally injured while he was being physically punished by his teacher. The culminating indignity was the calling of two policemen to the school who laid a ten-year-old boy on the floor in the presence of the administrator, teachers and children, handcuffed his feet and hands and then carried him out to the squad car.
>
> Earlier in the school year the principal had

remarked to me, "The children in this school seem so unhappy."

CHAPTER TWO

DEFINITIONS
(Adapted from <u>Corporal Punishment</u> in the
<u>American Psychologist,</u> Aug. 1974)

The word "punishment" comes from the same root
(L.poen) as do the words "penalty" and "pain." Thus we
may assume that semantically the relationship is of
ancient origin. "Cruel and unusual punishment" in the
Bill of Rights was intended to prohibit torture for the
purposes of extracting confessions or in retribution
for unlawful acts. Both penalty and pain are implied.
Webster's dictionary lists a number of metaphorical
uses of the word such as the deliberate punishment of
automobile tires to test their safety and endurance,
but as applied to human interactions, punishment means
"to impose a penalty for some fault," "to inflict a
penalty in retribution" or "to deal with harshly."
When punishment is prefaced by "corporal" (L.
Corpus - body), the meaning is unmistakably that of
pain upon the body of the person, usually by some
instrument such as a whip or paddle wielded by an agent
of the offended jurisdiction. For example, "Corporal
punishment was abolished in the Navy in 1850." In
California juvenile institutions, where corporal
punishment is forbidden, restraint is permitted, but
not the use of a strait jacket, gag, or thumbscrew or
by tricing up, stomping, arm twisting, washing of mouth
with soap, ducking, rabbit punches, curtailment of food
or by extremes of temperature. Comparable forbidden
school punishments would include, besides paddling,
such refinements as stuffing the mouth with paper
tissue, masking tape as a gag, shaking, ear pulling,
lifting by the hair, or throwing against the wall or
floor. Not definable as corporal punishment are fines,
discharges, loss of privileges and in schools:
detensions, exclusions and extra assignments.
In scientific endeavors it is common for new words
to be invented or for old ones to be given new meanings
to fit the needs of the new techniques. In computer
terminology, for example, common English words like

"bit," "word," "address," and "loop" have special
meanings within that particular discipline in addition
to their ordinary meanings. Thus when experimental
psychologists define punishment as "a reduction of the
future probability of a specific response as a result
of the immediate delivery of a stimulus for the
response, they are within the scholastic tradition
which permits the use of any combination of phonemes to
convey any concept, provided only that the terms are
defined and that the new definition gains wide
acceptance. The special definition of punishment as a
technical term in experimental psychology is thus
acceptable by these criteria.

The words "stimulus" and "response" used in so
redefining punishment have not themselves been as
carefully redefined from the common meanings.
Stripping them of the ordinary implication of
chronological sequence - stimulus first followed by
response - and assigning them meanings tied to the
status of the participants in which the experimenter
(high status) gives the stimulus and the subject (low
status) gives the response regardless of timing, has
gained wide but by no means universal acceptance even
among experimentalists. Uneasy jokes about rats
laughing among themselves at how cleverly they have
conditioned the white-coated human to provide food
indicates an awareness that the power relationship is
an essential ingredient in the stimulus-response
experiments and in the reasoning that follows them.

Special technical definitions are useful within a
discipline and among scholars who agree on the
unexpressed emotive load of the terms that are conveyed
without having either to state it or defend it.
Communication is expedited by the sense of exactness
these special terms convey, and the further exploration
of statistical parameters can be carried on free of the
doubts and hesitations that more philosophical and
semantically oriented phrases inevitably pose. The
laboratory term "punishment" is stripped of all
historical associations, all derivational implications.
No consideration of the intention of the experimenter
or of the feelings of the subject is admissible. The
idea of retribution, the law of the talon, the eye for
an eye prescription, all are outside of and irrevelant
to the pursuit of the scientific study of punishment.
Aversiveness is only implied, not stated. "Any
stimulus that reduces the frequency of the behavior
that precedes it," as the simplified version has it,
does not limit in any way what the stimulus might be
and does not require that it be painful or even
unpleasant. The only stated criteria is that it be

14

successful in diminishing or eliminating the behavior chosen by the experimenter as the object of the procedure.

Outside the special environment of the laboratory or seminars in experimental techniques, the stripped-down-clean meaning of punishment as defined by experimental technicians shivers naked in a world in which tradition, ethics, social policy, law, legislation, child rearing, deliquency, war, feuds, power, gambling, daredeviltry, ambivalence, masochism, and assorted evils and goods vie with the spirit of scientific inquiry and priority. Words used a technical sense in the laboratory are heard elsewhere as if embedded in another matrix. In the case of computers, if laymen conjure up visions of loops and bits gangling like tinsel monkey wrenches inside a magic machine, no particular harm is done. But in the case of punishment, the consequences of a dual vocabulary can be fraught with legal, medical, social and educational booby traps that range far beyond the narrow applications found in the literature on punishment in the laboratory sense.

A startling example of this is supplied by B. F. Skinner who wrote: "My name was being cited by both sides in a lawsuit in a southern city in which a school was being sued for using corporal punishment." Editorialized the Phi Delta Kappan: "Dallas public schools can keep the spanking rules they adopted after consultation with B. F. Skinner, the U. S. Supreme Court ruled recently." In actual fact, B. F. Skinner has opposed corporal punishment of school children. He has said,

Punitive methods of social control no doubt work. They would not have been so widely practiced throughout human history if they did not. But they have unfortunate by-products, which are quite obvious in the field of education. The student who is studying to avoid punishment will find other ways of avoiding it such as being truant or drop-out.

Punitive control may lead him to vandalize school property, to attack teachers and, when he becomes a voter, to refuse to support education. All these by-products can be avoided by turning to non-punitive methods.

In the City of Dallas, Texas, 24,035 instances of corporal punishment were recorded for the 1971-72 school year, some of them were so severe as to need medical attention and in several cases, hospitalization. Thus many thousands of children are subjected to punishment in the ordinary meaning of retribution and pain under laws that are defended, at least in part, by the laboratory definition of whatever will successfully change behavior.

The dual definition is shockingly sharp in the cartoon depicting a rat lab with the graduate student (with hair) saying to the professor (bald), "Incidentally, we'll be short one rat this morning. The black and white one bit me and I bashed his skull in."

In spite of the definition of punishment as whatever is effective, the problem usually set has been, "does it work?" An example: "The Effective Use of Punishment to Modify Behavior in the Classroom by R. V. Hall in 1971 is one of the few of this kind. After noting the "controversy among the proponents of behavior modification regarding the use of punishment" Hall and his assistants conducted four expriments using as punishment: finger pointing with a shouted "No!", withdrawal of name slips, staying after school, and after school tutoring. His finding was that "systematic punishment procedures which do not result in strong emotional behavior do have a general applicability to classroom problems." Quoted out of context the title and conclusion of his report could be quoted in defense of corporal punishment with "strong emotional behavior" assumed by the non-psychologists on the School Board to mean violent screaming, frothing and thrashing bout of limbs. Thus unless warned that, among other confusions, after school tutoring is being labeled as punishment in spite of the valiant efforts of educators to present it as opportunity, laymen may placidly assume that their prejudice in favor of old fashioned whacks has been confirmed by modern psychology. This enhances their approval of "psychology" but does nothing to increase their understanding of the effects of painful punishment on school children.

Similar misunderstanding has been caused by rapid reading of Donald Baer's article "Let's Take Another Look at Punishment" in Psychology Today (1971). Both Hall and Baer begin by defining punishment as "any consequence of behavior that reduces the future probability of that behavior," (Hall) or "any stimulus that reduces the frequency of the behavior that precedes it" (Baer). Both assume that corporal punishment went out with the gay nineties.

"Hitting misbehaving students with rulers or making students sit in a corner with a dunce cap on their hands were common practices in the **early days** of American education (Hall - emphasis added).

16

"I think that much of our revulsion regarding the use of punishment is based on a reaction against the truly inhumane conditions of **years ago** that recur in literature - headmasters with canes, slavemasters, prison turnkeys with whips, bullies, orphanage overseers, snakepit mental hospitals. We like to think of such practices as long past, so when the therapist speaks objectively about the uses of punishment, we react as if he were asking us to forget all the years of progress and reform" (Baer - emphasis added).

There are many Americas. In the kindly America in which these experimentalists must have grown up, children were taught without blows. The assumption that there have been "years of progress and reform" is one that many successful Americans make. Nat Hentoff who researched corporal punishment for the American Civil Liberties Union, began his November, 1971 Civil Liberties article with this admission:

If asked two years ago, I would have expressed doubt that corporal punishment was still an issue in our schools - except perhaps in a rural fastness or at the hands of a disruptive teacher who would be sternly warned by his principal not to beat a child again. Whatever the other failings of our school, at least physical barbarism - with its festering psychic residue - were safely locked into the past. Or so I thought.

"I was shocked out of my ignorance," he wrote as his research progressed. "Corporal punishment...is far from extinct. In a number of places most egregiously Dallas, the brutalization of children appears to be a part of the core curriculum."

In the vocabulary of legislators, corporal punishment carries the dictionary and popular meaning: Painful penalty as a consequence of the performance of a forbidden behavior. The behaviors so forbidden are defined by the teacher or principal of each school to suit his temperament and convenience. It may be anything from tripping a teacher to returning thirty seconds late after recess. It is given to high school senior girls for missing a class and to kindergarten children for "telling stories." Nor is it generally asserted that such paddling, punching, whipping, slapping, slamming or other battering will reduce the frequency of the behavior that precedes it. The boy failed to say, "Sir," therefore he has earned three blows.

A final critique of defining punishment as any stimulus that reduces the frequency of the behavior

17

that precedes it must address itself to that word "any." We have been reassured that punishment does not have to be painful, nor necessarily result in a strong emotional response, but otherwise no limits have been placed on what it might be. This cavalier attitude about "any" contrasts with the paucity of punishing agents recommended by psychologists and also with the traditional deprivations used by schoolmen. Let me suggest a few "punishments" that fit the approved definition by might not be so defined by the subjects. A hurt child's crying can be reduced with a kiss and an band-aid. An active child's jumping about can be reduced by placing a television set ten feet in front of him. The future probability of a mass exodus from the school grounds at noon could be reduced by providing free pizza in the lunchroom. Pouting and "I won't" behavior has been eliminated by assigning an underplaced child to a higher and therefore compatible grade level.

The choice of "punishment" or more properly the "corrective" depends on the reason for the behavior. Out-of-seat behavior, that bane of the teacher and popular choice for modification procedures, has been caused in one school district over a period of ten years by a fistula involving the coccyx, a recent whipping on the buttocks, pinworms about the anus, tight underwear, no underwear, a minor kidney infection, an undiscovered visual defect, boredom, inappropriate subject matter seen as insulting, (a story about white gloves at a girl's birthday party assigned to a Klamath River Indian boy), hunger, overtutoring, anxiety about a home situation (divorce, fire, brother arrested, illness of mother), a continuing feud, a mental set caused by overhearing much criticism of the school as being "too permissive; they let the kids do anything they want to."

Choice of "punishment" thus becomes the major task of the behavior modifier. The casual adoption of sweets or tokens as reward in all cases and the infliction of aversive stimuli such as a time-out box or the principal's paddle or other simplistic, narrow reductionism of "any" is not enough. Across-the-board one-menu-for-all methods are insulting and doomed to eventual failure. The search for an individual prescription to fit a particular child in a particular situation with a particular background and history does not need to be seen as an abandonment of learning principles. It does require a more careful observation of the whole field and an individuation of recommendations for corrective measures. Without such case study methods, "psychology" has merely substituted

18

one pain for another and punishment remains the fate of the powerless.

The use of the word "corrective" is high recommended in place of both reward and punishment as more accurate and as more likely to solve the dilemma of the ethical reservations of those who have learned to handle interpersonal exchanges without the use of force and fear, and, most important to all, to prevent the kind of misquoting and misuse of learning principles that flowed between Harvard and the U. S. Supreme Court, thus affecting the cultural lag of Texas.

CHAPTER THREE

PSYCHOLOGIST AND SPANKING

During the Sixties the dominant tone of experimental psychologists writing about punishment in their professional journals could be summed up as "Don't sell punishment short. It works."

The punishments they were talking about were electric shocks to make rats skitter through mazes, withholding of food pellets from pigeons who pecked the wrong spot and various painful prods at monkeys, turtles, cockroaches and other caged and compliant animals. Those who experimented with humans used captive groups: prisoners, alcoholics or college students, most of whom had good reason to go along with the project, or profoundly retarded or disturbed people confined in institutions who had no choice. Very few experiments used normal school children and those that did used such punishments as a pointed finger, the word "Wrong," "time out" - a version of go sit in the corner, or a strange invention called "white noise," an unpleasant hum of all the audible notes at once. In no case were experiments conducted that included spanking or other physical punishments.

The purpose of the majority of the experiments was to determine the most efficient way to apply the punishment. Timing, intensity, manner of delivery, intermittent scheduling and other technical tricks were manipulated in endless variations but no attention was paid to the effects, immediate, or delayed, on the animals, the prisoners or the pupils. The rat runners flipped the switch to shock the animal into action as casually as you and I press the the car starter. It never occurred to them, apparently, that in the wild the animals would scatter and escape rather than perform the unnatural antics required of them.

One of those rare ones who did observe the effects of punishment on the animals was Nathan Azrin who made careful observations to see what the rats did when the wire floor of their cage was electrified. Being a scientist he said they "emitted avoidance behavior" rather than simply that they tried to escape, but he was amazed at the ingenuity they used to nullify the shock. If a runway was available the rat scooted to safety, but if not, it would jump about trying other ways to avoid the pain. Standing on one foot broke the circuit an so did turning over on its back because the fur acted as an insulation. The cleverest rat had its picture taken for a textbook. It was titled "Breakfast in Bed." The smart little beastie discovered that it could lie on its back and yet press the food bar, thus getting food without punishment. For those who could neither escape nor avoid, the result was rage. The animal attacked anything handy: a tennis ball, an otherwise peaceable cage mate or even the iron bars of the cage itself. Azrin described it this way:

> ...Two rats were placed in a chamber containing a floor grid. In the absence of foot shock by the experimenter, the animals showed no signs of aggression. Upon the delivery of foot shock, however, the rats turned and attacked each other. This elicted aggression has been found to exist in several species and to be elicted by different types of painful stimulation.

Lastly when no other resource was left, the animal bit itself.

The parallel between this behavior and the behavior of human youth is clear. The first reaction is avoidance behavior. The child as well as the lab rat will try to avoid the pain. Running away, squirming, lying, blaming others, tightening the buttocks, the child will avoid, delay or minimize the pain physical punishment any way it can and, as we shall see later, the human has far more options than does the bred-for-tameness white rat. If escape is impossible the child, like any mammal, will become aggressive. Hurt children will attack their toys, dolls, pets, playmates and even their "cage," especially if it is a hated schoolroom and they have grown strong enough.

But this is not what the "punishment works" authors were writing about. They believed, naively as it turned out, that there have been "years of progress and reform" since the days of headmasters with canes and assorted adult bullies. The illustrations offered by the benign punishers of the Sixties were oftenest of adults who willingly subjected themselves to aversive behavior modification techniques in the hope of ridding themselves of phobias, fetishes and assorted bad habits. A seventeen-year-old girl sneezed without stopping for six months. Fastened to a wire and battery contraption, she spent four hours getting a sharp painful shock to her hand each time she sneezed. The sneezing stopped and we are let to assume that she lived happily ever after. Compulsive prying, the urge to molest young children, a yen for silk underwear and a wide variety of oddities were eliminated once and for all by a therapist who teams the unwanted excitant with an electric shock often enough to break the pleasurable connection. Then the patient was free from his fetish and able to make a more normal choice of love object. The claims of success escalated in stridency and excitement. The method was hailed as being as effective as vaccine, but only by the behavior therapist themselves. Their disappointment that they did no get nominated for Nobel prizes in medicine was laid to stubbornness and stupidity on the part of the unappreciative world who refused their "new and scientific breakthrough," in the science of psychology.

The truth was that those patients for whom it did not work announced themselves as cured rather than endure (and pay for) any more punishment. Those for whom it did work for a while were pronounced cured if they refrained from indulging themselves for six months or a year. After that, they disappeared into the vast sea of troubled people searching for a new guru, a new fad, a new cult, or giving up and living with their gluttony or abnormality with what equanimity they could. In other journals case studies appeared of patients who had been "cured" by aversion therapy and then had to be rescued from attempted suicide. Anorexia nervosa, (deliberate starvation) that had been "cured" by punishing failure to eat until the young woman had reached normal weight, was found more often than not to have recurred within a few years in an even more severe form. Weight loss achieved by aversive behavior modification was soon regained. And homosexuality, a favorite target for the modifiers came out of the closet with such fanfare that it was removed from the list of mental illnesses. The aversive modifers retreated to the institutions for the severely retarded, the severely emotionally disturbed, the self-destructive, and with their hand held inductoriums (shock rods) concentrated on eliminating teeth grinding, thumb jabbing and nail biting among the rejects of the human family whom nobody wanted and whose screams are unheard outside the thick walls of their institutional prisons.

The Seventies were approaching and with them the outcry about battered children. Dr. Ray E. Helfer and C. Henry Kempe edited "The Battered Child" in 1968 and "Helping the Battered Child and His Family" in 1972. Parents Anonymous chapters began proliferating shortly thereafter. Child Advocacy groups of many kinds sprang up including the well funded Children's Defense Fund whose special concern for minority children involved health and welfare as well as education. Congress held hearings and, led by then-Senator Mondale, enacted legislation setting up regional centers under a National Center for Child Abuse and Neglect. Stories of torture and murder of helpless children began to appear on the evening news. One little girl was found by the highway patrol clinging to the fence along a high speed freeway where she had been for ten hours. Skinny and frightened, she told police that her parents had put her out of the car and told her to stay there. They were traced and were found to have murdered another child before abandoning this one. They were jailed. A string tied around the penis of a baby boy resulted in his death. The body of a little girl was found weighted with rocks in the East River and the story of bureaucratic bungling that led up to this filled the news for week. The American public became highly conscious of burned, beaten, broken and battered babies and children. Debate raged over whether the perpetrators were psychotic or whether they might be ordinary people under severe stress and without a family network to help in emergencies. A change began. Hands raised in anger began to weaken on the downstroke as fear of accusations of child abuse became still small voices of conscience.

The last "punishment works" article appeared in 1872 in the American Psychologist. A lengthy techincal piece, it was replete with the same strident claims of success but salted and peppered with little knotty problems still to be solved because the findings were "mixed." It ended with a plea for more time to experiment before ethical judgments were made. But the time for nit picky quibbles over the precise degree of control and the adequacy of triple reversal designs was passing. The author admitted that "It is likely to be extremely difficult to control adequately the non-laboratory environment to the degree necessary to produce valid results." Educators who had welcomed the promises of sure-cure and had admitted the experimenters into the classroom to work on individual problem children began to run out of patience. The experimenters cluttered the space with their equipment and the air with their jargon while the other children and the teacher were distracted from the normal routine. The fine line, if any, between salutary correction and child abuse cried out for defining. Ethical judgments had to be made without benefit of scientific exactness. The aversive experimentalists among psychologists had monopolized the spotlight for a decade or more, but they compromised only a small percentage of the 50 thousand members of the profession. Most psychologists were engrossed in problems other than the matter of punishment and its effects and needed reminding of the older and more realistic psychological tradition.

Felix Adler in old Vienna was the first to set up community clinics and to offer general advice about child rearing. He strongly emphasized the futility of spanking. "Corporal punishment in childhood leads to low courage in adulthood," he wrote. His followers have continued to advise natural consequences - if a child gets his shoes wet in the snow, he must stay indoors until they are dried by the fire. This simple acceptance of the results of his actions teaches far better than a power struggle between parent and child. American adherents were similarly practical and direct. Hans Ansbacher: "The punished student will want to avoid school, to look for means of escape, not means of meeting the difficulty." And Theodore Dreikurs: "The punished shrug it off as the fortunes of war. Our classrooms are filled with acts of retaliation."

In his essay, "A Child is Being Beaten," Freud described daydreaming about spanking or being spanked as a fantasy to mastrubate by. His followers and those who built on his beginnings were even more specific.

The buttocks as the locus for the induction of pain is considered a safe locus. However, the anal region is also the major erotic zone at the time at which the child is likely to be beaten there. Thus it is aptly chosen to achieve deranged sexuality in adulthood. (David Bakan)

Trauma in childhood, including corporal punishment, may be associated with an interruption of normal sexual development and lead to numerous other forms of disorder. (Alexander and Ross)

Punishment may produce varieties of abnormal behavior such as rigidity, fixation, regression, aggression, displacement, primitivization and resignation. (Yates)

More on this aspect of the subject will be found in Chapter Five on Sex and Sadism.

Social psychologists found other disadvantages in the use of physical punishment. Sheldon and Eleanor Glueck studied 1000 delinquents in the Fifties and found that one of the common characteristics of aggressive youthful lawbreakers was a history of excessive punishment. Contrary to the popular opinion, they were not the pampered, do-as-you-please permissively raised spoiled brats. Instead they had been thoroughly beaten, neglected and had learned to duck and dodge authority from early infancy. Years of careful investigation yielded the same result: "Physical punishment was the favored disciplinary method of both fathers and mothers of delinquent boys." Their contemporaries agreed with the Gluecks. The English team of Bowlby and Burbin studied and wrote about "Personal Aggressiveness and War" in 1950. Their conclusion:

> Corporal punishment escalates; discipline becomes harder to enforce. More energy is spent policing as children develop deviousness. The 'bad boy' becomes the 'hero;' gangs form to defeat the teacher.

Later investigators repeated the work and came to the same conclusion: Excessive physical punishment unless neutralized by very favorable other circumstances injects a streak of cruelty in the character of the victim which may be expressed when he is grown without the law, or if in a position of power, within the law. Both cause much unnecessary suffering.

Among these studies are some that trace child punishment to its primitive origins:

> Maltreatment of children has been justified for many centuries by the belief that severe physical punishment was necessary to maintain discipline, to transmit educational ideas, to please certain gods or to expel evil spirits.

> From the schools of Sumer, 5000 years ago, discipline oscillated between abandonment of the rod to its use to the point of savagery. We are entering a new phase of our history wherein one of our most serious concerns is the protection of children. (Radbill)

Developmental psychologists who study changes over the life span concentrate on childhood for the most part and the relationships and impact of the environment as these effect growth and character formation at later stages. They have been unanimous in their findings that punitive parents produce poorly adjusted children.

> The child will do what the punitive parent demands only as long as he thinks that they will find out about his actions he may not follow their prescriptions at all if he thinks he can "get away with it." The parent relying heavily upon punishment must continually be on guard because his child is likely to rebel against his wishes.

We anticipated that punishment for aggression would lead to inhibition of aggression.... Field studies contradict these predictions.... Increased aggression was routinely found to be associated with increased punishment for this behavior. (Eron, Walder & Lefkowitz)

Other developmentalists spell out strong suggestions. Spanking episodes should be analyzed, parents are told:
We must look carefully, thoroughly and rationally at the experiences of childhood and we must come out forcefully against those experiences that set the stage for later bigotry, brutality and violence, the symptoms of essential contempt for other people. (Button)

Educational psychologists spoke out most explicitly. Basic texts such as those by Falk and by Cutts and Mosely went into great detail in their analysis of the social structure and the use of torture to maintain the power of one group over another. Both of these fine books trace cruelty through the ages and conclude with reasoned yet passionate appeals for the abolition of corporal punishment in schools. These texts were published during and just after World War II when the shock of the incredible Nazi concentration camps gripped the civilized world in a determination to eliminate official sadism for all time.

These quotations from Adlerian, Freudian, social and developmental and educational psychologists are typical of what psychologists had written. Each from their various angles had seen corporal punishments as an ancient evil from which civilized people must free themselves. That leaves only one major group, the apostles of the primacy of reward and punishment: the behaviorists. Perhaps they saw some good in spanking school children to make them learn, to enforce obedience or improve their character? Indeed they did not.
The Father of American behaviorism, John B. Watson, opposed whipping children for his own reasons. It is not advised, he wrote, because it "cannot be regulated according to any scientific dosage." As he saw it in the 1920's, "Punishment is either too mild to establish a conditioned negative response, or too severe, thus stirring up unnecessarily the whole visceral system of the child. It is either too rare to

meet scientific conditions or too frequent, thus making for habituation and masochism."

Nor have more recent eminent behaviorist changed that stance. B. F. Skinner, the most widely known name in American Psychology with scientific as well as popular books on the best seller list, from the top of the heap at Harvard pontificated that, yes, indeed it worked but condemned it nevertheless:

> Punitive methods of social control no doubt work. They would not have been so widely practiced throughout human history if they did not. But they have unfortunate by-products... It works to the disadvantage of both the punished and the punisher.

That did it. In the summer of 1974 at the height of the political scandal when wrong doing in high places made everyone feel guilty about too severely punishing wrong doing in low places, the subject of corporal punishment of school children broke through the barrier of silence and was openly argued. At the annual convention of the American Psychological Association a resolution against it was offered and debated. The experimentalists were able to save themselves a little room to manipulate by amending the whereas and inserting an exception of sorts for their small piece of turf. In January of 1975, the Council of Representatives in assembled meeting agreed to the following:

WHEREAS:

> The resort to corporal punishment tends to reduce the likelihood of employing more effective, humane, and creative ways of interacting with children.

> It is evident that socially acceptable goals of education, training and socialization can be achieved without the use of physical violence against children, and that children so raised, grow to moral and competent adulthood.

> Corporal punishment intended to influence "undesirable responses" may create in the child the impression that he or she is an "undesirable person;" and an impression that lowers self-esteem and may have chronic consequences.

> Research has shown that to a considerable extent children learn by imitating the behavior of adults, especially those they are dependent upon; and the use of corporal punishment by adults

27

having authority over children is likely to train children to use physical violence to control behavior rather than rational persuasion, education and intelligent forms of both positive and negative reinforcement.

Research has shown that the effective use of punishment is eliminating undesirable behavior requires precision in timing, duration, intensity and specificity, as well as considerable sophistication in controlling a variety of relevant environmental and cognitive factors, such that punishment administered in institutional settings, without attention to all these variables, is likely to instill hostility, rage and a sense of powerlessness without reducing the undesirable behavior.

THEREFORE IT BE RESOLVED; That the American Psychological Association opposes the use of corporal punishment in schools, juvenile facilities, child care nurseries, and other institutions, public or private, where children are cared for or educated.

Although the decision was not unanimous, very few psychologist spoke out against the adoption of the resolution. Some who were employed in school systems where paddling was a common as kleenex were mildly surpirsed, but most adapted with little difficulty. The dedicated behavior modifiers may have been a bit slower to do the double take necessary. They had to live with the ambiguity of having been taught that punishment works and finding that their top theoreticians had long before spoken out against the side effects among human subjects. Except for the aversive therapists who had so dehumanized the severely handicapped that they had no trouble continuing their treatments with cattle prods and other painful stimuli, only one or two certified psychologists reached print in defense of corporal punishment of school age children.

One of these is worth a hard look. It is well known that theories in psychology as well as in other sciences are shaped as much by one's character and attitudes as they are by what has been taught or learned from experiments. This example will suggest that in choosing a therapist it is wise to consider what kind of person you are talking to as well as where he was educated and what system of therapy he prefers.

At a convention of the Association for the

28

Advancement of Behavior Therapy this psychologist whom we shall provide with the alias of Dr. Tule Bochs, presented a paper titled "The Modification of the Pathological Behavior of the Adolescent Female Psychopath by the Use of in Situ Aversive Psychotherapy." It was billed in advance as "an important breakthrough in psychotherapy." He was called a "pioneer" who got "unparalleled results." He even wrote a book about it. What is not recorded is the true story of the trial and conviction of "Dr. Bochs" for child abuse.

The patient was not quite sixteen. She was placed in Dr. Bochs home to receive treatment by "a system of rewards and punishments." She remained there 17 days before being rescued by social workers after her bruises were discovered at school. The punishment had consisted of whippings and enemas. The whippings were administered with several types of instruments. These consisted of three paddles of various sizes and weights, a whip-like gadget constructed from a broom handle with leather strands studded with hardened balls of glue-like substance, a second whip-like instrument with leather strands, and a leather belt with a brass buckle. The indictment read:

On September 11, the defendant struck the victim with each instrument in order to demonstrate to her what punishment she would receive when she violated a prescribed rule. She was struck with the whip-like instruments and the belt on the rear and thighs while holding onto a bench in front of her in a standing position, legs apart, head down and completely naked. She was struck with the paddles while lying naked across the defendant's lap. The victim was struck on that day a total of 47 times.

On the following day, the victim left a note that she was going to the lake, but went instead to the store. For this she was punished under the same conditions described above by being struck on the rear and thighs a total of 37 times with the whip-like instrument studded with balls of glue-type substance.

On September 16, two enemas, consisting of four quarts of salted water, which the victim was required to mix, were administered for the purpose of demonstration. She was struck with a wire with a solder ball on the end of it when she was unable to hold the second enema.

On three subsequent occasions, the victim received punishments similiar in condition and severity to those described above. As a result of

29

these punishments, the victim had bruises evident
on her legs which alarmed members of the high
school staff. Her father was contacted by the
school principal; custody was transferred by
telephone to the principal and (she) was removed
from the defendant's home.

Dr. Bochs was arrested, tried and convicted of
child abuse. His appeals to the State Supreme Court
failed. He was given an indeterminate sentence not to
exceed nine months. He is no longer a member of the
American Psychological Association.

There are a few shysters in every profession. One
is wise to choose with care a lawyer, a physician, a
merchant or other supplier of goods and services.
Psychologists are no exception. They are not all alike
and they agree with each other even less than do
economists and stock market analysts. Most members of
all professions attempt to serve their clients well if
only because repeat business and word-of-mouth
referrals, usually known as reputation, make or break
their career. But a certain small fringe in every
profession is recruited from those with brains and
ability, but who were distorted, quite possibly by a
traumatic childhood, and whose phobias and fantasies,
residual fears and hatreds, leave an emptiness or an
insatiable hunger. They may function well part of the
time, or until their quirk intrudes. Then - may the
customer beware.

It is well to know the stigmata of the crook, the
criminal and the obsessive compulsive character, and to
avoid them as the plague. With psychologists as with
politicians, a fascinated dedication to control by
aversive means is the mark identifying danger.
Avoidance behavior is highly recommended.

The same is true of educators.

CHAPTER FOUR

MEDICAL CONSIDERATIONS

A survey of professionals and their attitudes
toward school punishment was made in Nova Scotia by Dr.
John P. Anderson of Dalhousie University. A random
sample of 703 physicians, social workers, nurses,
clergy, police officers, educators and lawyers were
asked: Should school teachers strap children for
disciplinary purposes? Not surprisingly the high
percentage in favor of retaining the strap was found
among educators. A Windsor schoolmaster made no
apologies: "A good caning never hurt anyone."
Opposition was greatest among physicians, clergymen,
nurses, social workers and media people. Only 19.9
percent of these said yes, retain the cane, while 74
percent said abolish it and 6 percent equivocated. In
reporting his findings for the Canadian Pediatric
Society, Dr. Anderson said that educators had been very
open and honest when they were asked if they had ever
come close to seriously injuring a child in their care.
He concluded with his personal recommendation:
"Strapping will help no child and should be abolished
from all Canadian schools."

In sworn testimony for the prosecution in the
trial of a teacher accused of using excessive force and
bizarre punishment, Dr. Moses Grossman of San Francisco
gave this deposition:

From the medical point of view corporal
punishment, unless very strictly controlled,
always involves the risk of bodily damage which at
times might be severe. This is particularly the
case when punishment is being administered in the
heat of anger - when the person administering the
punishment may not be fully in control of his
emotions and might apply more force than he
intended.

In my opinion any kind of blows on the head
must be absolutely banned. Any blow to the head
whether delivered by fist, open hand, book, or
results from being shoved into a wall can result

31

in the production of either an epidural or subdural hemorrhage.

Similarly choking should have no place in the methods of punishment used. Choking can result in the decrease of the supply of oxygen to the brain, or might even result in vomiting and aspiration of vomited contents into the lungs.

Blows about the chest, over the gentilia and kidney areas might also produce unexpected and serious physical difficulties.

Punishment which is capable of producing such injury should simply not be allowed. Although blows upon the buttocks have been knows to cause broken blood vessels, massive fat emboli, and sciatic nerve damage, it is generally thought to be the safest area because no vital organs are located there. This, of course, presupposes that the skin is not broken and that the genitals are protected.

Other medical men have issued similar warnings. Dr. John Caffey of Children's Hospital of Pittsburgh, Pennsylvania warns, "Kids are not cocktails that need to be shaken to be good." He elaborated:

A child's head is relatively large for weak neck muscles and violent shaking can cause neck injuries or burst blood vessels in the young brain. Bones of legs or arms can be broken from the shearing action of the movements. The whiplash shaking is a precarious, pervasive and pernicious habit which can be observed... in the home, on the street, in buses, nurseries, kindergartens, day care centers, orphanages, preschools... Permanent damage to brain or eyes, mental retardation or death can result.

The skull and brain structure of the infant and small child are more vulnerable to damage than most people suppose... Vulnerability varies inversely with age. Male infants are twice as vulnerable as females, probably due to the relatively slow maturation of male heads and brains.

An orthopedic surgeon, Dr. Frederick L. Goodwin of Portland, Oregon, was asked to review and give an opinion on a school paddle that measured 33" long including a 17" handle. The base was 10" across and almost an inch thick. It weighed 4 pounds. Twenty-six holes, each the size of a penny were drilled through the base. Dr. Goodwin refers to it as a "so-called paddle, more in the category of a club or a semi-brutal

32

weapon. He said:

From an orthopedic standpoint this would be considered a very dangerous weapon... There are multiple reasons for this. The length of the paddle would give it such leverage that the impact on the buttocks of a child could be such that it could give him several of the following: 1. It could cause a subdural hematoma from the contracoup effect. 2. It could cause particular hemorrhages in the brain from the same type of traumatic jar, as well as subarachnoid hemorrhages. 3. In reference to the gluteal muscles of the buttocks, it could do considerable damage to these and to the underlying bones of the pelvis. 4. If the paddle did not hit quite sharply and was turned slightly obliquely, this paddle could cause severe damage to the sciatic nerves in the gluteal area... If it happened to hit in the right place it could cause a fracture of the bones of the pelvis and/or the femoral femur.

If the above is not enough, it could knock even a grown adult of my size, something like 200 pounds, off his feet and the damage could be multiple if the child was knocked off his feet to the floor or into a wall.

The above considerations and opinions are given at this time: 1. As a human being with consideration for other human beings, 2. As a father in consideration of children, and, 3. As a professional orthopedist in consideration of true medical injuries which could result from such an instrument.

Dr Eli Newberger testified in a case involving a ten month old baby boy enrolled in a day care center in Prosperity, South Carolina, whose crying was deemed to be merely attention seeking and who was given "cracks" on the butt by the principal in charge. As Director of the Family Development Study of Childrens Hospital Medical Center in Boston, Dr. Newberger examined the child and found that he had been exposed to substantial risks of permanent injury. The seven "cracks" he took could have resulted in a broken spine rendering the infant paraplegic or in a fatal hematoma of the abdomen or in a ruptured spleen.

The testimony of these doctors given in court, before legislative committees, to school boards and to their colleagues cannot be dismissed as sentimentality. As health professions they are appalled at the casual use of potentially dangerous weapons with no safeguards against possible mistakes or emotional imbalances on the part of the child and/or the punishing adult. The doctors are the ones who have to pick up the pieces. In the doctor's office came Joseph Desimone who has impaired hearing, his parents claim, because the assistant principal of the Plymouth Junior High in Philadelphia struck him on the side of the head. In Norfolk, Virginia, a P.E. teacher is being sued for $200,000 for a partially severed thumb. During a punishment drill in which the whole class was ordered to attach one offending student, the victim fell, caught his thumb in a door which slammed on it and cut it half off. Although she had a pass in her hand, Tami Joy was caught and accused of cutting; the paddling brought on a nervous rash, a change in her menstrual cycle, continual stomach cramps, diarrhea, a new tendency to bite her nails and school phobia. Jose N. was wearing a helmet to protect an opening in his skull from recent surgery. Nevertheless when he was naughty the teacher hit him on the head. In Arlington, Texas, Chip V. was walking too fast down the hall. He was yanked back by the principal and dragged down the length of the hall. As a result he suffered from a separated cartilage in his shoulder. J. C. Blivens suffered a broken arm as the result of the brutality of the principal of the Ervin School in Dallas, claims his mother. A six foot, 190 pound teacher allegedly put his whole weight on a ten-year-old in Tonawanda, New York while he hit, slapped and pounded her head on the floor. But most of the cases are welts and bruises on or near the buttocks. Sometimes even doctors have been knows to suggest that this is less damaging because there are no vital organs on that part of the anatomy that "nature has seen fit to provide."

Having a thorough knowledge of anatomy, however, doctors know that this is not entirely true. A closer look at that part of the body might make people aware of the complications in the place that it doesn't hurt to hurt. The gluteus maximus, the muscle that takes most beatings, in the subject of jokes, scatological and Rabelaisian. Even the sound of the name, **gluteus maximus**, is enough to get some to giggling. The bruised boy sets off hilarity rather than pity. "Ha! 1 bet he won't sit down for a week!" Yet when called upon to defend the practice, a mere sting to the skin, temporary and benign, is described and defended as the total effect. Even the angriest threat "I'll take the skin off your butt," assumes that damage is limited to replaceable epidermis. But the truth is that the underlying tissues, muscles, blood vessel, nerves, cartilage and boney structure are inevitably involved.

The large size of the gluteal muscles, maximus, medius
and minimus, is one of the most characteristic points
in the muscular system of the human as contrasted with
other mammals because this is what enables us to stand
erect. Standing up on two feet was the first ability
that separated the human from lower forms of life.
"Standing on your own two feet" is still metaphorically
the distinctive sign of the truly autonomous person.
With damaged gluteal, this becomes difficult. Observe
the painful walk of the recently beaten child. His
trunk is bent forward to a simian angle; his arms hang
limply and each step is an effort. In severe cases he
may not be able to walk at all. Norman L., a small and
some said sassy 12 year old was taken out to a quonset
hut that doubled as a storeroom and "woodshed" in a
northern California school and was beaten so badly that
when he crawled home, his mother thought he had been
hurt by an automobile. He could not straighten up.
The skin was not broken, yet the damage was deep and
severe.
     The blood supply to this part of the body is
through large and small vessels, the iliac and femoral
arteries and veins and their branches and tributaries.
These are the blood vessels that split and spill their
contents into the surrounding tissue, between the
muscle fibers and under the skin when beatings or other
injuries make purple bruises. Subcutaneous hematoma
commonly result from paddling especially from glancing
glows from the edge of the paddle. In the case of
familial abuse, a child died from repetitive beatings.
The skin was gone from both buttocks but the corner was
interested to learn how a child could die from a
spanking, especially in a so-called "safe" place. An
autopsy was performed to discover whether the injury
had penetrated to any depth, and if so, what damage had
been done internally. Incisions were made; hemorrhages
and scars were found threaded all through the muscular
tissue. Death had been caused by an emboli, a bit of
clotted blood or fatty tissue that had entered a broken
blood vessel. It was small enough to flow along
through the larger veins but when it reached the tiny
capillaries of the heart and brain it formed a dam that
prevented further blood from reaching the affected
part. Circulation being stopped in both heart and
brain, they starved for oxygen and nutrients and ceased
fuctioning. Death ensued.
     The nerve supply to the hip region is particularly
rich. The spinal cord ends well up in the lower back;
from there the nerves fan out in an elaborate network
making for a highly sensitive area. The sciatic nerve
that lies fairly close to the surface as it runs down

35

the back of the leg is particularly susceptible to injury and inflamation. Dr. Barris who was the school health officer in Dallas reported that he had seen a boy with a permanent atrophy of one leg due to sciatic nerve damage attributed to a hard blow with a paddle administered over the buttock area. The genitals, even if not directly hit are necessarily jarred and stimulated. Sometimes the injury is direct although inadvertant. Many young boys have an unevenness and torsion of the lower testis may be caused by a paddling or by the sudden tightening of the muscles in anticipation of the blows. The Sanford, Florida schools are quick to paddle for any and all offenses and, for tossing jelly beans and small stones at a head on school grounds, four boys were routinely punished. Within half a hour one of them was on the operating table. Dr. Gonzalo Hauman who performed the operation said that the paddling had contributed to a congenital condition. During the paddling, he explained to a reporter for the Sanford Herald, one of the testes twisted 60 degrees, cutting off blood flow and causing excruciating pain. He untwisted the injured testis, sutured both, thus preventing the problem from recurring. The incident caused quite a flurry of publicity.

Commenting on this, Dr. Albert N. May of Ohio said, "I am sure that the Dean of Students who administered the paddling never intended to cause such serious injury to the youngster; however, when physical force is applied to the child about whom the current health status is not completely known to the adult, this kind of unintentional injury will occur from time to time."

Less direct and immediately obvious damage due to the proximity of the reproductive system to the sit of punishing blows is only slowly being admitted. Sadism and masochism, impotence and distortion of choice of sex object are traced directly to the association of pain with awakening sexual sensations. This will be dealt with in more detail in Chapter Five.

The bony structure of the hips include the coccyx, the residual tail bones. It is subject to being broken off from any sudden slam such as a drop on a teeter tauter or having a chair withdrawn unexpectedly when one is about to sit down as well as from a hard paddling. This can result in a troublesome system among other difficulties. Even more vulnerable is the vertebral column, the back bone. Lower back pain is the second most common complaint - the first being headache - that plagues the human body. "Oh, my aching back" is a joking synonym for overwork and weariness.

The cause of this weakness has been blamed on evolution. Our simian ancestors walked on all fours, this theory claims, and when humankind stood up, an unnatural pressure squeezed the cartilage between the vertebra causing injury and pain. But all that happened millions of years ago. It is possible, indeed likely, that there is a more immediate cause. Battering on the backsides during the growing years may result in an unnatural jarring, pinching dislocation of the cartilaginous pads between each vertebra, starting a degenerative process that many years later, under strain, is felt as a painful backache. As long ago as 1927, J. A. Chresomales, D. C., PhD, wrote: "Spanking children on the buttocks might cause an injury by misplacing the tail end of the sacral bone, thus possibly producing a harmful spinal curvature."

"Reaching the brain through the seat of the pants" sounds like a joke and is usually said with a chuckle, but can be an accurate description of what happens as a British instructor was aware. He was accustomed to explaining to new members of the faculty: "You got to make them feel their arse hole up behind their back teeth."

The bend over position children are required to assume to accept the blows insures that the force will travel the length of the spinal column along the chain of boney enclosures for the neural path from the legs to the brain. If any of the openings for nerves are twisted or any cartilaginous pad slips, there can be years of un- or mis-diagnosed trouble. The whole profession of chiropractic is built upon the undeniable fact that Americans have back trouble.

The strange folksy-cutsy cliche about there being no vital organs there ignores the fact that the most vital of organs is exactly right there. If the organs that produce new life are not "vital" then nothing is. The mystery and miracle of birth from this most despised site had confused our morals, our customs and our thinking. How could the portal through which each of us entered this world be considered the place most appropriate for the infliction of pain by the stong upon the weak? It becomes still less comprehensible when we realize that it is legal in most states for an adult male (his sexual hang-ups unexamined) to batter young women of child bearing age without regard for their physical condition at the time.

It was the medical profession that uncovered the hidden horror of child abuse. Infanticide is not new but public concern about it is. Children subjected to corporal punishment are at risk of early death. But

37

most don't die. Some live with brain damage; some live with enlarged adrenal glands that make them feisty, trigger happy, fearful and vicious.

Dr. S. H. Frazier, psychiatrist at Columbia College of Physicians and Surgeons, found in his study of murderers that they had been victims of remorseless brutality. As children they had been choked, thrown through glass doors, stripped naked and beaten and put out into snow drifts. The other fact of childhood for them - 90 murderers from Minnesota and Texas - included early exposure to guns and alcoholic parents. These were rural children turned killers. City children were found by Dr. A. H. Green, Professor of Psychiatry in Brooklyn, to turn out much the same. Child abuse points to later criminality, they agreed. Dr. Joel Fort, Professor in the School of Criminality at the University of California interviewed and studied such infamous murderers as Charles Manson, Edmund Kemper, Tex Watson and others. His conclusions;

"From many years of work as a social and health problems specialist, including a unique opportunity to evaluate mass murderers and serve as an expert witness at their trials, I have found parental neglect and physical abuse to be a very common threat of their childhoods."

Doctors have known this for a long time. In 1958, the Journal of the American Medical Association published a piece called, "Etiological Factors in First Degree Murder." Dr. Glen M. Duncan wrote: "Among six prisoners convicted of first degree murder, remorseless physical brutality at the hands of parents had been a constant experience for four of them. The other two were psychotic."

Torture is not too strong a word for "remorseless physical brutality." We know very little about the long term effects of torture. The common assumption is that as soon as the pain stops, given a while for the obvious wounds to heal, the victim is restored to life whole and able to take up where he left off. That's the foreshortened version on film. In the real world, this ancient, barbaric form of persuasion is a closet phenomenon that we prefer not to have to deal with. To confound us, periodically a survivor rises from the ashes of the torture heap and tells us again what it was like. We read, shudder and resume our comfortable assumptions. Amnesty International, however, is taking the position that it is not enough to rescue the victims, but that the permanent physiological effects merit study.

Dr. Derek Richter of London concluded that the long term effects of torture are practiced upon political prisoners present medical science and society with an increasing challenge. "In addition to chronic anxiety, physical deformities and depression, torture victims may suffer paranoia, early aging, withdrawal from reality and increased vulnerability to tuberculosis, alcoholism and drug abuse." He does not mention children, but the after effects he catalogued include some of the most troublesome debilities of adolescents. Vulnerability to alcoholism and drug abuse certainly describes the condition of far too many young people and they have been studies extensively for almost every variable that could account for the condition without supplying definitive answers. The connection between drug abuse and child abuse seems to have occurred to very few; only now (1977) is there beginning to appear an interest in researching this probable connection. Such studies might profitably start with the strong medical evidence demonstrated in the work of Hans Selye of McGill University.

When the human or animal is under stress from cold, worry, disease, infection, overwork, intense excitement, pain or other strain, the body reacts in predictable ways. It may do special things to combat specific injuries but always an additional three things happen: The adrenal cortex increases in size, sending more hormones into the blood; the thymus and lymph glands shrink; and the lining of the stomach becomes red and irritated, in extreme cases bloody or ulcerous. This, Dr. Selye calls the alarm reaction. It calls into play the main regulators of the stress syndrome: the brain, nerves, pituitary, thyroid, adrenals, liver, kidney, blood vessels, connective tissue cells and white blood cells. The body is mobilized to maintain itself and to fend off, destroy or otherwise neutralize the intruding stressor. Thus when three-year-old Jeffrey Klein was paddled at nursery school for the serious sin of taking another child's lollypop, the imprint of the paddle remained on his buttocks that evening. When he cried and vomited at the dinner table, his mother tried to help him, but he push away and, grabbing his bottom, ran blindly into the wall. Alarmed, she called her husband. Between them, they gently eased Jeffrey into a warm tub and examined his bruises. (For the story of the trial see Chapter Seven.)

"I only intended to cause a sting," said the principal. "I used only a wrist action, not my arm. After the first swat he stomped his feet and cried the cry of a spoiled brat. After the third swat he quieted down and turned it off."

Jeffrey was three-years-old. The "sting" that

reddened his buttocks, left raised welts and burst blood vessels had caused subcutaneous hematoma, but it had obviously done more than that. The stress had set off the alarm reaction and spun the baby into the first stage of the general adaptation syndrome which Selye defines as the "bodily expression of the generalized call to arms of the defensive forces of the organism." Adrenaline poured into his blood stream giving rise to expressions of fear (crying) and anger (stomping his foot). Resistance of the whole body was coordinated; the thymus (growth gland) shrank, white blood cells doubled and gastric acid poured from the lining into his stomach. These somatic reactions, however, were not competent to deal with the wicked paddle which appeared life threatening to the child. The next reaction after two more blows was quite different. The punisher thought he had finally pounded some sense into the recalcitrant little imp and that of his own free will he had decided to obey the command to be still, but Selye's stress syndrome hypothesizes a quite different series of events.

There are three stages of adaptation to stress; alarm, resistance and exhaustion. In the first, chemical alarm signals are sent by the painful part to the centers of coordination in the nervous system and to the endocrine glands, especially the pituitary and the adrenals which produce adaptive hormones to combat wear and tear on the body. But no living organism an be maintained continually in a state of alarm. If the damage is so extensive as to be incompatible with life, then death ensues during the alarm reaction within the first few hours. If survival is possible at all, the second stage, that of resistance, follows. The body adapts to the stress and appears to be in a state of equilibrium. This adaptation is tenuous however; under continued stress this acquired adaptation is easily lost. Fresh stress may send the organism into the third stage, exhaustion. "At the end of a life under stress there is a kind of premature aging due to wear and tear."

The Selye experiments with laboratory rats using cold as the stressor showed that they could adapt to near freezing temperatures after an original alarm reaction, but that additional stress was poorly born and after several months they lost their ability to withstand cold even in moderate amounts. Similar experiments using other stressors such as intense prolonged exercise or toxic drugs gave the same results. After a certain amount of stress came an adaptation to it and an apparent ability to withstand it without harm. This made it more difficult to adapt to a still greater level of stress and eventually they dropped into a third stage with total exhaustion and inability to cope.

Unlike battered children who reached stage three and either die or live on for short brain damaged lives, Jeffrey was rescued after he reached the second stage; his parents withdrew him from the school. During the second stage, a sort of numbed shock, he seemed to have adapted to the requirements of a stressful situation until he attempted to eat his supper. His mother did not say whether she had threatened to spank him if he did not eat his supper nicely and thus we cannot be sure just what in the immediate situation reactivated the alarm. In any case, the normal supper situation with whatever minor stresses it usually entailed could not be handled by a child already in stage two. Fortunately loving parents became aware that something was seriously wrong; their expressions of sympathy and determination to safeguard the child, along with the warm bath eased him way back to - or very close to - his normal self.

Some boys, usually older than Jeffrey, are said to be so used to spankings that they don't understand anything else. The battering has not been severe enough to injure them conspicuously, but it has been prolonged enough to keep them in the second stage of adaptation to the stress. This too helps to explain the contradiction of juvenile delinquents who appear "tough" on the surface, yet fall apart easily. The slightest criticism is heard as deadly insult; the explosive impulsivity, the lack of self control are not character traits so much as they are adaptations to excessive stress. The return to baseline for Jeffrey was possible; return for others to what society might consider acceptable behavior may very well be impossible after a point of no return. Selye concluded that each human is endowed at birth with a finite amount of adaptation energy which may be spent conservatively over a long lifetime or expended rapidly in high excitement and early death.

Correcting by pain is a hazardous habit especially when carried on by men who may not be aware of their strength or their mood of the moment, who use an instrument that does not provide feed-back regarding the amount of force they are using as might an open palm since it too stings in response to a slap or spank. Usually too they are unaware of the physical health of the child they are punishing and unaware of his stage of adaptation to physical punishment and the effect that another stressful situation may produce.

Far safer and better in every way is to avoid any

possible damage whether physical or psychological and
to maintain decorum and high morale by non-violent
means.

CHAPTER FIVE

SEX AND SADISM

In 1962 some unsophisticated rural educators still considered psychology synonomous with sex. Thus when the principal of Endeavor Elementary School in stunningly beautiful but off the beaten track Shasta County was confronted with a school psychologist for the first time, he had no idea how to make use of such an esoteric offer of help. He rubbed the back of his neck in perplexity.

The school clerk frowned with him. "Maybe you could refer Alec? He's been at it again."

He beamed in relief. "Okay. You can test Alec." He dropped the paper like a dose of poison he thought he might have to swallow. "You make out this form on him, will you?" The clerk was used to picking up the pieces after her boss. He jammed the paper into the machine upside down, snapped her gum and tried again.

Alec proved to be an exceptional boy. Large for his twelve years, probably a bit of a bully, the test results showed normal intelligence and the usual year and a half below grade level in reading. Denying all difficulties, he asked no questions after being reassued that, no, he didn't "haf to," but splinkled appeasing "sir's" and "ma'am's" at irregular intervals. There seemed to be no special pathology except the endemic passivity and slyness I had met and been baffled by a number of times before in this closed community.

The clerk had not typed anything under "Reason for Referral," but she told me over coffee in the teachers' room what the real complaint was.

"He's homosexual!" she gasped and broke into embarrassed giggles. "Couldn't you tell?"

"Oh?" I said. "What happened?"

"The parents have been complaining. You see, the kids get off the bus at Six Corners and they have to walk the rest of the way. They live along that road. We kept getting phone calls. The mothers kept calling up telling us to make him stop pestering the little girls. Well, he got paddled for that for a while and finally he stopped. Then he starts pestering the boys."

"Pestering? How?"

"Oh, you know. Teasing. He kept trying to kiss them." She flushed. I couldn't help wondering if she was trying to hint at childish sex play. It was clear that she thought she was talking to someone who could read her mind and could tell that she had shameful dreams, the first psychologist she had met.

"He was paddled for kissing the little girls? In broad daylight on the walk home?"

"Yes." She gathered courage. "And then he starts kissing the boys!" Her embarrassment turned to stern indignation. "What are you going to do with a kid like that?"

I was as shocked about the paddling as she was about the kissing. Her silent demanding stare had to be answered although this was neither the place nor the person for a serious conference. I made a offhand remark that I was to regret.

"Well, paddling isn't going to help."

The incident was only one in a series of cultural clashes between the erudite learning inbibed at the University of Chicago and the crude reality of the fundamentalist enclave that had carried the rod of correction like a religious icon on the grand trek from Oklahoma a generation before.

The County Superintendent was running for reelection and had to make hay of whatever he could. He knew his people and their predilection for a juicy scandal and a handy scapegoat. Hung on the grapevine was the rumor, all too eagerly believed, that test scores secured by the psychologist were reported directly to Moscow. When the Red should invade the lumber slopes they would already know which families could be brainwashed and which would have to be shot. The "homosexual" remark provided the coupe de grace. A seven point headline, picked up by the Hearst newspaper chain, spread the one day shocker across the country:

SPANKING CAUSES HOMOSEXUALITY EXPERT SAYS

Naively indignant, I denied I had said any such thing. No one listened. In fact, no one in the community spoke to me. This bothered me less than the label, "expert," that I did not merit since I know almost nothing about spanking, its effect upon scholarship, emotions or mental health. About homosexuality I had only such knowledge as could be gleaned from a single short chapter in a text on abnormal psychology dated 1943. I did have a certain expertise I believed with troubled children and

44

educational problems, but to be labeled "expert" when I was merely amazed made me humbly aware of how much more about human nature I had yet to learn. There was nothing for it but to resign and flee to that haven of comparative sanity, Berkeley. A summer of unemployment made it possible for me to haunt the library, fill the gap in my education and discover that the headline writer, whoever he may have been, had a great many experts in his corner. I have wondered if he was widely read or widely experienced.

I turned first to Freud. His description of three erotic stages, oral, anal, and genital, and the character traits that were supposed to be shown by people who never fully progressed to the adult (genital) stage had never made sense to me. The anal erotic was retentive, both constipated and greedy for gold? Smokers were satisfying some oral urge never consumated in infancy? These and similar exotic notions did not square with my experience and didn't help me solve children's problems and I ignored them. Now in the summer of 62, still shaken from being, as I thought of it, run out of Shasta County, I poured over the original essays.

Freud's essay, "A Child Is Being Beaten" did not enlighten. It was an analysis of a remembered childhood, not a child. His patient was haunted by the fantasy of a child being beaten, and after many pages of subconscious guilt about love for mother and murder for father, it seemed that the young man patient was using the fantasy to mastrubate by. Elsewhere, however, Freud was brief, but quite explicit:

> An erogenous source of the passive impulse for cruelty (masochism) is found in the painful irritation of the gluteal region, which is familiar to all educators since the confessions of J. J. Rousseau. This has justly caused them to demand that physical punishment, which is usually directed to this part of the body, should be withheld from children in whom the libido might be forced into collateral roads by the later demands of cultural education.

"Collateral roads?" Yet he did seem to be saying, however obscurely, that physical punishment should be withheld from children. My respect for Freud rose a not in spite of the irrelevencies. The mention of Rousseau, whom I had not read, reminded me again of my illiteracy. How can a person go through college and get a master's degree and be so unfamiliar with what the thinking minds of the past have to tell us?

In his Confessions, Jean Jaque Rousseau tells that

he was a motherless but much loved and unspanked child until the age of eight when he was sent for schooling to the home of a minister whose sister inflicted the usual punishment:

> For some time she was content with threats and this threat of punishment that was quite new to me appeared very terrible; but after it had been carried out, I found the reality less terrible than the expectation; and, what was still more strange, this chastisement made me still more devoted to her to inflicted it. .... I had found in the pain, even in the disgrace, a mixture of sensuality which had left me less afraid than desirous of experiencing it again from the same hand. No doubt some precocious sexual instinct was mingled with this feeling.... Who would believe that this childish punishment inflicted on me when only eight-years-old by a young woman of thirty, disposed of my tastes, my desires, my passions, and my own self for the remainder of my life?

I was learning. But why had one of this been required reading for a degree in educational psychology?

Leopold von Sacher-Masoch, the German novelist and Comte Donatien Alphonse Francios de Sade, the French soldier, made nineteeth century Europe aware by their writings that these strange dimensions of sex were neither new nor uncommon. They gave their names to the sexual aberrations that require pain, given or received, in order to achieve release. This might involve the same or opposite sex, it mattered little. Pain is the excitant; sensation without esteem for self or partners the result.

Beating and whipping experiences in childhood are closely linked with sexual deviations in adulthood. This is as true for those who come to prefer cruelty to others as it is for those who enjoy being hurt. A child abuser confessed during a psychiatric interview with his therapist:

> There is no pleasure so pleasurable as the pleasure of another's pain. But one cannot get away with it completely... I am frequently burdened with remorse... I feel especially guilty that I sometimes get an erection and even climax during the beating. This is vile and hurts me dreadfully.

The underground press turns this shame into an enticement to patronize the specialist. The Berkeley

46

<u>Barb</u>, when it was an amalgam of political protest and pornography, included a pullout section devoted to kinky sex ads. Many of them promised the sadistic enjoyment of spanking:

"If the whip is your trip, call Randy."
"English Mistress provides lessons in discipline!"
"Let me show you the ropes."

A correspondent in Pennsylvania direction my attention to S.A.N.D. Ltd. a publisher of spanking erotica in Scarborough, Ontario. The blurb on the back page of the paperback reads:

Spanking for Passion or Punishment? What erotic preliminary need is served by the reddening of plump bottoms, the birch marked thighs? The spanker needs it for physical arousal; the spankee for the awakening of slumbering passions.

Among a wealth of stories, one describes a school teacher, 38, stocky and severe:

Five years ago my nephew who was then 14 spent his summer vacation with me. He was quite a mischievious boy and one evening when he was in his pajamas I rather angrily took him over my knee for a hairbrush spanking. I spanked him quite soundly and to my surprise he developed an erection during the workout. In the weeks that followed I was quite surprised to find that he would often deliberately disobey me in order to be spanked, and that he always got an erection while squirming around on my knee.

What was pandered illegally in plain wrappers yesterday is news today. In these times of openness and candor what was hidden shame to the Victorians is exposed to the public press for all to read. It is reported that the Public Records Office in London has released after 75 years under lock and key, the information that the four times Prime Minister Gladstone was addicted to the whip. "Had it been sufficiently considered," he wrote on pages decorated with squiggles of thonged whips, "how far pain may become a ground of enjoyment?"

George Orwell whose dire predictions about the world of 1984 were based in large part in his residual impressions of the classrooms of his youth, describes the beatings, at first with a riding whip and later with the more painful rattan cane that were reserved for the boys whose fathers made less than 2000 pounds per year.

Jenny Churchill, the American mother of Winston Churchill, was appalled by the treatment of English schoolboys. The headmaster of her son's first prep school turned out to be an incredible sadist. When Mrs. Everest (his nanny) showed Jenny the marks of the constant beatings Winston had received, he was promptly removed and sent to a better school in Brighton.

Direct sexual exploitations of children is almost universally abhorred. Even in prisons where the varieties of criminality stratify the inmates into a rough pecking order, the child molester is despised as the lowest of the low. Embezzlers and strong arm burglars will not associate with them. A prominent clergyman proposed that they should be castrated, although he apologized for it later. The suspicion that a child molester haunts the neighborhood is enough to give nightmares to parents and to keep children housebound until he is captured. Of all the kinds of child abuse, the hurtful use of a little one as a sex object is the most unforgivable.

Yet for all our horror we seem blandly aware that battering at the buttocks of a child, presumably for disciplinary purposes, partakes of the same elements of sex and sadism. "The rump is aptly chosen," noted Bakan in his discussion of anal erotism, "to achieve deranged sexuality in adulthood."

If there lingers any suspicion that this is merely theoretical speculation with no provable connection between spanking and distorted sex preferences, that doubt is dispelled by the publication of Ian Gibson's The English Vice by Duckworth of London in 1978. Over 300 pages of tightly packed research beginning with a seventeeth century German, who recommended flagellation as a cure for impotence and who referred back to a fifteenth century Italian who suffered from an inability to have an erection except after flagellation and had so suffered from childhood. There follows case upon case, authority upon authority, some repeated in detail from original sources, others sketched in briefly. The early sources are from all over Europe but twentieth century data are mostly English. The civilized nations abandoned the whipping of school children, but the English clung to the custom with a tenacity worthy of some better aim. They still do. Even Germany gave it up, restored in under Hitler and have abolished it in schools officially and in homes to a certain extent.

It was from France that there came the first serious attempt to persuade the government to ban the beating of children. Francois-Amedee Doppet in 1788 published a small volume on "External Aphrodisiac" which explained that children punished thus became sexually aroused, begin to enjoy beating each other and to mastrubate. The interest becomes an obsession and as an adult the victim finds he cannot fulfill his marital obligations without being whipped, makes his wife miserable and finds relief only in fustigation by prostitutes. He was outraged at teachers who, by beating their scholars, enflamed their passions and turned it into unnatural channels. He even realized that teachers enjoyed the duty far too much and that alternatives have been knows since Rousseau. French teachers got the message. Doppet deserves primary credit for the ending of corporal punishment in French schools.

Gibson notes that English medical men also wrote of flagellation in the nineteenth century by that William Acton who wrote the most widely read text in 1857 became more concerned about masturbation than about whipping. He set about to warn of the dangers that followed from this indulgence. The Victorians carried this hypocrisy to such extremes that women were accounted as having no sexual feelings and men patronized whipping brothels in great numbers. Eton and the famous schools for upper class English gentlemen considered bare bottom caning as a "natural incident of the day." The poet Swinburn, whose ribald poetry is quoted at length was obsessed by it.

English educators did not get the message. According to Gibson, they continued to enjoy "swishing" bit I find it difficult to believe that bare bottom birching continued to be practiced at Eton into the 1960's and for all anyone knows may be still.

The British Psychological Society authorized a working party on corporal punishment in schools. Their report issued in 1980 concludes a section on "The Psychopathology of Physical Punishment" with an understated warning:

Advocates of corporal punishment in schools should examine very carefully the weight of evidence now available and, particularly in the light of the pornographic component, consider whether they can justify the continuation of a system with such a capacity for exciting unhealthy interest. This is not to cast doubt upon the motives of the punishers themselves, which in most cases may be reasonable and unobjectionable, but rather to take into account the dangerous effects that beating has upon certain impressionable children and adults, and the potential for cynical exploitation.

There is also the question of the very small minority of teachers who come to light in out cases from time to time who are certainly unfit by reason of their temperament to have the opportunity of inflicting corporal punishment available to them. One may question whether sufficient safeguards exist in the teaching profession to control the activities of such persons. Teachers at present receive no screening for loss of self control under stress or sexual deviance before entering into the profession, and any attempt to introduce an effective screening programme would be met with sound practical and ethical objections. The simplest solution would be to remove any temptation from those who may be unable to resist it.

CHAPTER SIX

RACE AND RACISM

Because he did not freeze into motionless silence while his teacher gossiped, a Chehalis Indian boy was welted across the small of his back and had his shirt torn half off.

The same teacher struck another boy about the head and face then picked him up bodily and thrust him head first into the garbage can and beat upon his buttocks while the boy struggled for breath.

The jury exonerated the teacher at both trials. He is back in the classroom today. A leather strap punched with stinging holes, fastened to a wooden handle is still in use at that school The parents cannot afford a civil suit and the only agency that cares is the Human Rights Commission. If society decides to protect the Chehalis Indian boy it will be, not because is a child half the size of his attacker, but because he is a "minority."

It is widely held that minority children suffer more corporal punishment than do White children. It has been documented that they are disportionately subject to suspensions and expulsions. Children Out of School in America, a publication of the Children's Defense Fund finds that "three-quarters of all children not enrolled in school are White. Proportionately, however, non-White children are out of school far more than White children (6.0% compared with 3.9% not enrolled respectively.) "Although no reliable counts have been made of the race of those children subjected to physical discipline, the chances are good that the proportion is much the same.

Racism is a subtle concept. If it means an amorphous preference for our own kind, we are probably all guilty. It is refers to an irrational inequality in the imposition of blame, American fairplay requires that it be raised to consciousness and be compensated for. Unless we are scrupulous, any "other" appears more faulty. Differences in customs, games, teases, jokes, pitch and accent, reticences, a thousand

51

cultural details, all may appear as disturbances, discourtesy, or in some way needing discipline.

It is doubtful if the Anglo disciplinarians in Chicano communities for example are aware of their attitudes. The cultural clash makes Spanish oaths seem more defiant than home grown curses; unfamiliarity makes shyness appear as stubbornness or stupidity; fear mistakes casual kidding for aggressive attack. For these and similar reasons, the tendency is to escalate the harshness of the penalties when the lines of authority and the expectation of submissiveness are drawn too clearly along racial lines.

It was thus in Guadalupe.

Dark green rows of broccoli stretched endlessly across the flats between the dry mountains and the ocean beach on a windy, westward jutting bulge in the California coast. The people of Guadalupe, 85% of them Mexican-Americans, work on the land and in the packing sheds. The town is a mile and a low hill from the Pacific, but tourists pass it by for Santa Barbara and Malibu farther south or Big Sur to the north. Anglos own the land, the sheds, the trucks; they run the town, the newspaper, the schools. Not until Cesar Chavez began unionizing the farm workers did a spark of pride ignite that enabled them to believe they could expect anything less demeaning. The growers worried. A speaker from an ultra-conservative organization was invited to address the townspeople. Some highly negative references to Chavez and the UFW were greeted with subdued boos and a few sibilant hisses. Less than a week later, ten Mexican-Americans were arrested for disturbing the peace at the school house meeting. Among those given a jail sentence was Sammy Gonsalez. The Los Angeles Times told his story:

Sammy did the right things. In his teens he worked packing and stapling and making cartons, while he finished Guadalupe's highest grade - the eighth - and attended high school in nearby Arroyo Grande. Each weekday he drove 20 miles to and from Hancock Community College in Santa Maria and put in six more hours boxing broccoli. But instead of being pointed out as an example of how to make it in an Anglo world, Sammy went to jail. For the reporter from Los Angeles, Sammy recalled his school days: "We got the pain, the bent fingers, and the bruises on our legs. The sons and daughters of important people...could sass the teachers, could get away with anything."

"What happened, Sammy?"

"I remember one day in sixth grade. It was ten minutes to three. I was doing some math drills in front of the class, and I kept getting mixed up, so the teacher made me put my right hand on the desk. Every time I said a wrong number, he whacked my hand with the side of the ruler. At 3:15, I still couldn't get the answers right and my hand was swollen and purple. I asked for permission to change hands and he let me. For the next twenty minutes - even after the bell rang - the teacher kept whacking me. Finally he let me go at 3:35. I couldn't close my fingers, so I had to pick up my books with my elbows. I cried all the way home, and I hated that teacher with all my heart."[3]

The California Advisory Committee to the U.S. Commission on Civil Rights [4] came to Guadalupe. Rather than complaining of their working conditions, the Mexican-American parents told how their children were abused.

Ricardo was six. His teacher wrapped a jump rope around him and his chair from above the elbows down to his hands so hard it left red rope burns.

Joey, 4' 10" tall and weighing 95 lbs. was punched in the face and his eye blackened for being the last one in, although the tardy bell had not yet rung. He said, "I was afraid to complain to the principal because they don't believe the kids and it doesn't do any good. I think they'd punish a Mexican kid for complaining, but it would be different for an Anglo kid."

Rene has trouble with her right ear. "I never had any trouble with it before that teacher blew the whistle right in my ear. It was in the cafeteria and we weren't supposed to talk, only whisper. You would never know when they were going to blow the whistles. A teacher with black hair blew the whistle very loud into my right ear. I didn't know it was coming and it really made me jump. All of a sudden my ear started buzzing. It also made my heart hit very hard and I didn't feeling like eating. When the wind blows like it always does in Guadalupe my right ear starts buzzing. The school nurse tested me and I couldn't ear the buzzer she put on. I didn't tell my mother because I was afraid she would send me to a doctor. It hurts lots of times and feels like the steel bar is rung in your ear. I tried to make it go away by putting my hand over my ear. But it won't when the wind starts blowing."

Irene, 3' 5" tall and weighing 55 lbs., was shaken and her hair pulled the first day of first grade.

Ruben, in fifth grade, was paddled for forgetting his history book and shaken for "talking." He said, "He took me with both of his hands on the top part of my arms and started shaking me violently about ten or eleven times. My head smashed against the wall and

really hurt. Then he lifted me out of my chair and
threw me against the wall. A metal hanger was sticking
out and it hit me in the back. He held me up in the
air after he thew me into the hanger and let me drop
very hard into my chair. This made my back hurt even
more."

Javier declared, "I was laughing and Mr. L hit me
very hard with his good hand..."

Good hand? Meaning what? After the formal
hearing, we heard the real horrors. Mr. L was a
veteran and had lost a hand. His prosthesis was a
metal hook, pirate style, which he used to carry his
brief case, move furniture, and grab errant boys by the
scruff. Only once did the hook catch the flesh and
tear a boy's shoulder. It had come close enough to the
jugular to frighten even himself. Thereafter, he used
only his good hand on the children.

Another off-the-record tale involved a scene in
the boys' bathroom where one had run for sanctuary
after being overheard using a Spanish curse. In a
bizarre perversion of the customary mouth washing with
soap, the teacher had lifted the nine-year-old bodily,
turned him upside down, thrust his head into the toilet
bowl and held it there while he flushed it. "Three
times!" the lad insisted. For complaining about this
disgusting episode, his father had been threatened with
the loss of his job and his uncle with deportation.

The State Senate Select Committee on Children and
Youth held hearings. Mervyn Dumally, later to be the
first Black Lieutenant Govenor of any state and now in
Congress representing a part of Los Angeles, listened
sympathetically to the children recite their woes, to
the parents, to adminsitrators from nearby towns who
described how they managed the same kind of children by
giving them responsibility and holding them
accountable. He listened with understanding also to
the Guadalupe teachers who complained that it was all
exaggerated and they were being defamed for no good
reason. It just happened to be a very special day in
American history for those in positions of authority
who whined, as did one of the members of the School
Board that "it was a conspiracy, part of the Chavez
movement to upset everything." Accusations of
revolutionary intent on the part of people and
protestations of purity of motive on the part of those
in authority went down badly that day. Just before the
hearings resumed for the afternoon session, the radio
crackled the news of the resignation under fire of then
vice-president Agnew.

One of the psychologists who testified to the non-
productive effects of corporal punishment, Dr. Seymour

Feshbach of U.C.L.A. reported later; "...As the afternoon progressed, and Chicanos approached us with expressions of gratitude and Anglo teachers approached us with expressions of hostility, the realization grew that the debate over corporal punishment was but a minor expression of a profound conflict in the community between the Anglo establishment and the Chicano farm workers who, although a majority in number, are a minority in power and economic status. The Anglos control the farms, the major stores, and, of course, the schools. Opposition to corporal punishment implied support for Chavez, and, at a more fundamental level, much of the support for corporal punishment rested on racist attitudes toward Chicano children."[5]

A suit filed by Rural Legal Assistance resulted in a voluntary change of policy. The roughest teacher was fired, several others left; a new superintendent was hired and for a while at least, peace reigned.

It was not an isolated incident.

Unlike Gaudalupe, Madera is not a one-vegetable town. The lush vineyards of an irrigated Eden are cut by a roaring thoroughfare, Highway 99, then the main north-south artery between Mexico and Canada. The east-west artery between San Francisco and the mountain resorts and the gambling tables of Nevada bring another kind of traffic.

Here there were jobs in variety and abundance. If a youth prefers to escape stoop labor, he can try for a job at a gas station, in one of the many motels, eateries and truckers' havens or in the other small industries. The Anglo-Chicano population mix is closer to 60-40 and the schools are integrated. Agri-business is there and dominant but mainstream America has tempered the feudal overlordship with the counterweight of civil rights. Thus, the polarization is less simplistically between the White haves and the Brown have-nots. Next to the UFW verses the Teamsters/Growers the primary stand-off is between the Parents' Council and Los Padres Unidos, but there are defectors from both sides. This is what happened:

The swimming pool is the social center of the High School campus. Outdoors, unfenced, it induces a festive country club gaiety during the long, hot summers that begin in March and last until Christmas. It was June. Danny Salas was 16 and ready to tease himself a girlfriend. Dressed in shorts and halter, she was eager to be teased. She came up laughing when he pushed her into the water and the friendship might have rocked into bonding except for the shocked interference of the physical education teacher. Mrs. H. ran to her husband, the vice-principal, who ran after Danny, who fled in dismay. One interrupts courting behavior of the young at risk of overreaction by everyone. Danny was caught several blocks away where he "took a stance," they said, and thus justified his forcible capture and return to school, a bloodied and badly bruised boy. Danny weighed 114 lbs.; the men 350 lbs. collectively. Danny was bitterly denounced not so much because he had indulged in horse play at the pool, but more because he had **DELIBERATELY** smeared the clean white shirts of his captors with blood from his broken nose. A charge of battery was filed against the two men by the District Attorney, but two months later they were judged by a jury of their peers and found not guilty. The right of White adults to beat up Brown youth under the age of 18 had been vindicated again.

The Mexican-American community did not like the verdict. They had not been represented on the jury and feeling ran high. A picket line formed with placards, <u>Justice is Color Blind</u>. Letters to the Editor overflowed the <u>Madera Tribune</u>. "Disrespect for Law and Order." "Dr. Spock Permissiveness!" "Waste of Taxpayer's Money." Anglos gathered under the Parent's Council demanding that the picketers be expelled. Chicanos joined Los Padres Unidos with counter demands. Fringes screamed "revolutionary plot" on the one side and "racist oppression" on the other. Daily the picket line was reported as shrinking, but every day it was still there. The town was rent along ethnic lines.

What would have happened if the sixteen-year-old son of the town banker had teased and tossed the doctor's daughter while both were safe in an ethnic enclave country club, velvet lined with money and the security of membership in the dominant culture? Obviously nothing. No one would have demanded that he identify himself; he would not have needed to run; no one would have chased him, punched him in the face, bloodied his nose and mouth, thrown him on the ground and carried him back bodily to the clubhouse to be disciplined. Why then was this an appropriate response to horse play at the school pool when minority youth were involved?

Farther south, just under the southern mountain guarding the entrance to Los Angeles, the City of Bakersfield swelters in desert heat and simmers with racial distrust that boiled over one spring toward the end of the Nixon era when it was still assumed that unrestrained force, secret plans and cover up were the way to keep the rabble in order. Police used live bullets to break up a melee, and put three Chicano adolescents, one as young as 13, in the hospital with gunshot wounds.   At the high school, discipline is brutal and protests are handled by flying accusations of "Revolution."

Los Padres Unidos were courteous:

"We want to make it clear that if any students were violating the law we are not condoning it. However, we are very much disturbed about the way in which this incident was handled...

"We are very much concerned if we as parents were to treat our children in the same manner in which these students were treated, we would be jailed.

"But we are expected to sit back and applaud as strangers beat them, give them black eyes, lumps on the head, throw them around by the hair, kick them and twist their arms... You must remember our children are the most precious things we have and when you hurt them, you hurt us."

The tension between Anglos and the Chicanos is, of course, economic with the established growers guarding their lands and their genes against the encroachments of the pickers and packers who yearns for their share of the American dream. The drama is muted among adults who now depend largely upon boycotts and legislative dickering to gain their objectives. The violence that cannot be used against the union, given American labor strength won long ago, is deflected onto the children in schools. Under these circumstances, to allow Anglo administrators to use goon tactics on children is dangerous indeed. Chicano parents are aware of the special risks their children run in attending such schools, yet, at the same time earnestly desire that their children shall do well, learn English and be accepted in the larger society. Their opposition, thus, is not so much to physical punishment of the young which they themselves use upon occasion, as it is the likelihood of racial strife making scapegoats of their little ones and escalating the punishments to grotesque degrees as in Guadalupe, Madera and Bakersfield.

A poverty spread of Black Americans in an inner city ghetto is even more vulnerable to the imposition of excessive punishment on their children and they are similarly divided and ambivalent about such punishments. Without the strength of a union like the UFW to back them, they can be put down one by one. Helplessness, when pushed too far, may burst in strange and futile ways. This is what happened to "Myrtice Jones," a pseudonym, of course, but a very real person.

Big sisters are to be believed when they tell little brothers in first grade that they should stay away from the office. "They'se gonna keeel you!" Shirlette knew. She had been strapped hard across the hand for crossing the street at noon to buy pizza for lunch. When she impressed upon Rocky that the office was pure murder for him and to stay away from it, he believed her. When one day he was ordered to the office for running in the hall when schoolrule insisted WALK even to escape a bully, he knew it was a matter of life and death, so he cut for home. The playground teacher caught him by the arm, and though he struggled to get free, she held tight and marched him to the office. Shirlette saw the scuffle and ran home as fast as fourth grade legs could run. "Mama! They'se pushing on Rocky again!"

Myrtice Jones, just home from her 6 a.m. to 2 p.m. shift at the hospital, would have collapsed in total weariness and resignation except for the urging of her daughter and her mother, both of whom looked to her as breadwinner, head of the family and righter of all wrongs.

"You gonna let them kill him this time?" her mother demanded. "First they put him in that school with the crazy ones, now they beating up on him again. You better go see. And you put a stop to it, hear?"

"Mama, I seen that teacher. She's always pickin' on Rocky. She don't like him none. She grab him round the neck and carry him in that office. They's gonna keeeeel him!"

Myrtice pulled herself together and started for the school, her anger growing with each step. They had told her Rocky was emotionally disturbed and that he should be in a special school. They persuaded her that he'd get a lot of extra attention and that he wouldn't be so shy, so she had signed. But Rocky didn't like it. He cried all the time he was there. They had some crazy system, she told her mother, that they called "rage reduction,"* but mostly it meant they changed the rules every day for the special purpose to make sure the kids learned to obey. It was called the Honor School and that sounded nice, but after a while, she couldn't stand to hear Rocky's complaints. One day he told her that they threw him out of a moving car and that's why his trousers were torn. She hadn't believed him, certainly not, but still, she did want to talk it over with someone. No one would listen. The principal had said she's have to talk with the director of the special school and anyway, Rocky was only going there

*Rage reduction was subsequently censured by the professional organization of psychologists. It is no longer used.

58

half a day and he was doing so much better, so why bother? The director of the special school was never in on her days off and finally she had said to take him out and put him in regular school. Now, here they were beating on him with that big wooden paddle, big enough to swat a grown boy, but not too much for Rocky. Anyway, Rocky was a good boy. Shy, that was all. By the time she reached the school, she had talked herself into a mild fury.

The police report of what happened next is cold: "At approximately 1425 hours, while I was in Room #3 teaching reading to witnesses #1, #2 and #3, the door to my classroom opened and suspect Jones came into my room, shouted, YOU ARE NOT GOING TO BEAT UP ON MY KIDS, grabbed at my hair. I broke loose and said to suspect #1, "now just a minute," and I started for the door to get help. Suspect #1 picked up a chair and swung it at me. I put my left arm up to shield my face and I was struck on the arm by the chair that suspect Jones had swung at me."[9]

The teacher, young and inexperienced, had had no training in how to deal with angry parents. She knew all about vowel values but very little about human values as they were experienced by Black mothers. She had not personally been beating up on Rocky, but she had sent him often to the principal hoping he could do something to motivate the silent child to join with the others in learning his lessons. She was only dimly aware that the principal had one solution for all boys sent to the office. They were required to take hold of a chair back and bend over. The chair back was necessary because he found that merely bending over to touch toes as he used to have to do as a boy was not enough support. These little Black brats would fall over on their faces for the slightest swat.

The principal, demoted from a junior high because of parent complaints, was unhappy with his present placement. He could see no purpose in integration and often wondered to himself if there was any use in trying educate Black kids at all. Naturally, he called the police.

The D.A. had had some dealings with the Black Panthers and he knew a conspiracy when he smelled one. Myrtice was living proof that they had enlisted the women to mass assault the White teachers and he knew his duty was to defend them, the schools and the American way of life. He demanded that she be sentenced to a year and a day in prison for aggravated assault.

The probation officer reported that Myrtice May Jones had never been in trouble with the law before,

59

that she had been on welfare only briefly and was the sole support of three children and her mother. She did not drink, did not possess a gun, went to church regularly and was held in high esteem by her employer, the Community Hospital. Furthermore, he wrote, the school had tried to help her with the younger boy's problem, but this had not been successful.

At the hearing, Myrtice wanted to tell the judge about how they strapped Shirlette because there being no bread in the house to make a sandwich one Monday morning, she had given her a quarter and told her to buy a slice of pizza for lunch. For doing what her mother told her, Shirlette got cracked across the knuckles three times and made her hand so lame she couldn't do dishes. And she wanted to tell the judge about how they told her that Rocky had some disease called Autotism or something like that, and what they had to do was hold him down real tight until he got mad, and how scared he was of the men at the Honor School and how maybe he fell out of a car going from one school to the other but nobody would talk to her about it or explain how his pants were torn.

But the probation officer said, "You just let me handle this and we'll have you back home again in no time. You just don't say anything and it will be alright." So Myrtice said nothing, and the judge said, "Probation, one year with good behavior." And they told her she'd have to report once a month and not carry a gun and not bother the teachers any more.

Myrtice was grateful but she couldn't help gasping indignantly, "Where'm I gonna get a gun?"

The new school psychologist retested Rocky and decided he was not autistic but found that he was only five and should have been in kindergarten instead of first grade. His mother, in desperation because he had been put out of Headstart when she got off welfare and went to work, had lied about his birthdate so he could go to kindergarten. At four, he had not done well in reading readiness and had been overwhelmed with the demands made upon him. In first grade, at five, he was still not ready for reading and, because of his confusion, had not opened his mouth for the first two montns. He was listed as "without speech, probably autistic-like symptoms; recommend to Honor therapeutic sessions part-time." Now he is repeating first grade in a new school and because the newspapers had carried a story abut the teacher attack, everyone is a bit afraid to correct him. From being too shy, he is getting a bit forward, and he grins every time he overhears, "Cocky-Rocky."

It was all unnecessary. It gives credence to

60

those who claim that Black children take the brunt of the school battering. In integrated schools with unreconstructed White teachers, they do.

But there is another side to the question. Are Afro-Americans harder on their children at home? It is true that severe parental punishment is so much greater among them that their children "don't understand anything else?" There may be some justification for such statements. When asked what they would do if a five or six-year-old did not obey instantly, 20% of White parents replied that they would "spank until he couldn't sit down" or "hit him with the belt," but 67% of the Blacks said they would be that rough, sometimes or usually. Among Whites, poverty and poor education made a considerable difference, the poor and less educated being more ready to use violence than those who had some college or who had a middle class income. Among Blacks, however, there was less difference. Having grown up in the South also predisposed both Black and White to be quicker to punish severely.

This attitude apparently carries over to the schools. "If you can't hit them, you've got to put them out. That way they are denied an education. This plan to forbid spanking in school is a racist plot....!" said a southern Black educator in an excess of frustration One can sympathize with his determination that Black students must not be denied an opportunity to learn, but at the same time deplore his limited options, his unfortunate belief that he had only a choice of two evils.

At Mott Junior High in the Bronx, N.Y. two coaches with temporary appointments were named deans of discipline and stalked the halls with a "smoker" hurting and humiliating the students, sometimes offering them a choice of licks or suspension, and if they braved the licks, suspended them anyway and then, to top it off, thoroughly enjoyed their jobs and special prerogatives, grinning and laughing as they swung the smoker and stepped on fingers. All the participants in this tragedy were Black: the students, the deans, the principal who appointed them and the Citizen Commission who investigated. Also involved were the NAACP, the Metropolitan Applied Research Center whose Kenneth B. Clark noted that "some Black parents sought to justify the use of corporal punishment even as they were denying it was used."

This was "Black on Black" with a vengeance. Well intentioned people are left with a dilemma: Is Black self determination more important than children's rights? And is Black self determination fairly represented by people whose first concern seems to be

61

that they be given supervisory positions regardless of their qualifications? This is racism in its simplest form: the interchangeable parts theory. Assuming that all members of any group have the same characteristics and that anyone is qualified merely by birth is as racist as assuming that no member is qualified. The cooler heads of the Citizen's Commission agreed that the temporary deans were not qualified and that the President of the Parents' Asociation who doubled as aide to the principal was not a credible witness when she defended her employer while claiming to represent parents, saying, "It doesn't happen and besides they deserve it."

In Boston, on the other hand, abuse of Black children by Irish teachers was exposed by Jonathon Kozol's block buster, <u>Death</u> <u>at</u> <u>an</u> <u>Early</u> <u>Age</u>, and something was done about it. Not only did the rattanning in the basement cease, but changes were made in the demeaning aspects of social studies texts that presented minorities as inept, sneaky, dirty, inconsequential or only as props and scenery upon the stage where the Cabots and the Lodges strutted in solitary importance. The successful abolition of corporal punishment in Massachusetts lay in the willingness of people to listen, the motivation of middle management people to set up boards of inquiry, of media people to present the matter on television as news, and of legislative aides in the various governing bodies to formulate bills that their bosses are willing to take a chance on introducing.

Thus, racial concomitants of corporal punishment have two antithetical aspects: 1. The victimization of minority children, and 2. the folk beliefs held by many ethnic goups about their cultural heritage.

The first of these is surely true if one includes all poor families among the minorities. Poor rural and migrant Caucasians are held in low esteem and generally are as beleaguered as the inner city non-Whites. The second aspect of differential punitiveness among races needs further discussion.

A Chicano educator, principal of a school attended by his compatriots, is a member of the Human Relations Committee of his State Teachers' Association. His little power base is out of the mainstream and does not suffer from cross cultural conflicts. He was aghast at the thought of abolishing the spanking of children when the matter came up for consideration at a convention.

"Among our people, that's the way we do it. We spank our kids. It's part of our cultural heritage. You can't change that!" he was genuinely, naively, upset. Everyone in the room turned to look at him. "I don't knock them black and blue or anything like that. But our kids, if they need it, they get it. That's the way their parents want it. They tell me, 'If my kid don't behave, you spank him.'" He repeated, shaking his head in disbelief that anyone should challenge what to him seemed as inevitable as tacos and refried beans. "It's our culture. That's the way we do it."

His sincere conviction that the way he handled children was a special ethnic trait of his group sounded strangely like the nursery school supervisor who was asked why she permitted aides to hit children. "Among these people," she whispered - we being the only Caucasians in a Black gathering - "that's the way they do it. They strap their children. It's a part of their cultural heritage." She cocked her head knowingly. "I don't spank them. I wouldn't dream of it. But if you interfere with Black culture, you're a racist."

The same sentiments in almost the same words came from the fiercely set jaw of the doggedly independent Okie whose blue eyes and faded hair were standard in the beautiful Blue Mountains. Here casual cruelty to children is a matter for hilarious laughter. The paddling principal grinned. "Don't tell me how they do things in Los Angeles," he said, believing apparently that it was different there, which it was not. "Up here we don't take no guff from kids. We aren't paid to take any lipping off. It a kid gets smart, he gets clobbered. That's the way we do it. It's our culture, you might say. You can't change that."

Poor Brown, poor Black, poor White, all the dispossessed, the traditionalists, the authoritarians in awe of power and having none, squelch their children with blows. They are proud of it. The women who find it difficult, grip their resolution and "do their duty" since otherwise their children would be "spoiled" and would wind up lipping off the law. They hold no higher aspiration for their children's future than that they should stay out of jail. Each is ignorant of other ways and convinced that they alone in their ethnocentric purity know the right way, and that all others are in a conspiracy to weaken the fibre of the "character" they have beaten into their young, as they themselves were beaten.

The story of Mr. Charlie and Popsicle Pete is usually only in that the principal who told it was openly amused at his solution to the problem of punishments suited to three classes of students in his school. Many American educators have the grace to be ashamed of their punitiveness. Not so the wielder of

Mr. Charlie.

"This," he said, swinging a 24" paddle of plywood with his initials drilled in holes through the center, "is Mr. Charlie. If any of the big bullies from the other side of the tracks gets out of line, he gets it. They know it. In fact, they ask for it. I've tried giving them a choice of swats or detention, and they choose swats every time. It's over with in a hurry and they go out knowing they's paid for their fun and they feel better."

"Now this," he went on holding up a studded ping-pong paddle, "is for the middle class boys. They're not so tough, but they overstep bounds every so often. It stings enough to remind them to think twice next time."

Then he laughed. "This," he dug about in his desk drawer among the pencils and paper clips, "is Popsicle Pete." He brought out a tongue depressor. "I used to have a real popsicle stick, gut now I use this; they're about the same size. This is to slap the wrists of the Lakeside boys." He sneered. "If I ask them swats or stays, they choose detention every time and then Mama drives down to get them."

He was surprised at my astonishment. "You mean you openly treat boys differently depending on where they live."

"Sure," he said defensively. "I try to go along with what the parents want. That's good public relations."

Whatever the merit in catering to neighborhood customs and whatever the fault in abdicating leadership in child rearing, it is probably true that there is greater reliance on spanking among poor families than among the better educated. In Black Rage, Greer and Cobbs trace the origin of child beating:

"Beating in child rearing actually has its psychological roots in slavery." The loving Black parent wants her child to survive. Under the circumstances of slavery, to survive required avoidance of uniqueness, of pride, of manhood and the acceptance of shame and pain as the natural state of affairs. "The child is admonished to obey the teacher...and the teacher is urged to exercise parental prerogatives including beating. In this the parent yield up his final unique responsibility, the protection of his child against another's aggression"... "As parents urge (the teacher) not to spare the rod, that same parent is telling volumes about the life that child had led up to this moment. The parents tells of a child both beloved and beaten, of a

64

child taught to look for pain from even those who cherish him most, of a child who has come to feel that beatings are right and proper for him, and of a child whose view of the world, however gently it persuades him to act towards others, decrees for him that he is to be driven by the infliction of pain."

"Pity that child."

The native African mother does not beat her child; she suckles him until he is four or five. The Native American mother does not beat her child; she swaddles him safely in a papoose cradle that hands from her back or from a convenient branch so that safe from snakes and other marauders, he swings to the rhythm of her walking or to the gentle winds. The Oriental mother does not does not beat her child; shaming, family pride and respect for ancestors is sufficient to socialize the young.

Beating in child rearing is thus seen as a corollary of the life of the slave, the peon, the dispossessed in an emerging industrial society. In Czarist St. Petersburg, the father of the Anarchist firebrand-to-be, Emma Goldman, beat his daughter unmercifully. The accumulated fury kept the childless Emma embattled against the police and raging against injustice all the rest of her life. Her father was only slightly more brutal than his peers at that time and in that place. Shall we then say that child beating is a Jewish cultural tradition and you can't change that? On the contrary, the freedom and opportunity that America afforded the Jewish immigrant of a hundred years ago changed his child rearing customs from physical to verbal prods and to a concern that has made "Jewish Mother" a synonym for too much caring, too much protection. When there is fault, urging the young to achieve tends to be jawboning rather than bone crushing.

If any ethnic group can claim this peculiar custom of beating on the buttocks as its own, it is the English. In England and in its former colonies: Canada, Australia, New Zealand, South Africa, and most ubiquitously, Ireland, the cane is used extensively in the schools although it has died out elsewhere in Europe. It was banned in Poland in 1783, reinstated under the Russians and banned again in 1918, ended in Holland in 1850, in France in 1887, in Finland in 1890, in Norway in 1935, in Sweden in 1958, in Denmark in 1968, and in most of Germany after Hitler. It is not used in the Soviet Union or any of the countries of Eastern Europe. It is not used in Israel, nor in

65

Japan. Only the English cling to the Roman rite of the
absolute power of the pater familias and his deputies,
with education by rote enforced by the ferule. Asks
Londoner Peter Newell, member of STOPP (Society of
Teachers Opposed to Physical Punishment), "Are the
British such a violent and uncontrollable people that
they are unable to do without a sordid, degrading
sanction which a large part of the civilized world has
successfully be able to abandon?"

    Whether cause or effect or both, caning, an
attenuated, symbolic castration, performed in dual
function. It taught "place," that is total subjection
with gratitude for being allowed to live at all. Most
canings were for "cheek" or "general cheekiness," or
for in some way challenging the authoritarian rule of
the master. This teaching was a strong form of
regimentation since an avowed purpose was to make the
boys all alike, to hold the same values, to memorize
the identical data and above to be loyal, to the school
and each other. A sort of bonding process, difficult
for the outsider to understand, binds the boy to the
master as, in an almost atavistic leige lord fashion he
becomes subject to him and to the school. As explained
by Mercurio in a study of Boys' High in Christchurch,
New Zealand, "...the ritualistic, even tribal character
of the phenomenon. ...Caning can be seen as something
of a ceremony, a rite of passage, an almost mysical
bond that ties boys to one another, to their masters
and to the school, and moreover, it does these things
in ways which an outsider would be hard-pressed to
appreciate." The boys boast to one another that they
can take "six of the best" without a whimper; any boy
not caned risks the disesteem of his peers, is called a
"goody-goody" and definitely does not belong. It is a
highly masculine rite, in which the attainment of
manliness is marked by being tough enough to take it
without a whimper or a show of emotion of any kind. It
is, thus, in its first function, a conservative force,
designed to keep the social structure intact and to
inspire fealty to the powers that be and keep each
uncomplainingly in his place. In defeats social
mobility, discourages ambition of better one's self,
eliminates independence of judgment, stifles ability to
adjust to changing conditions, and squelches any hint
of the valuable critical, creative thought. It raises
a breed of obedient killer soldiers of whom Kipling
could rhaposidize:
                "Their's not to question why,
                 Their's but to do and die."
    The second function of caning in the English
tradition was to train colonial administrators in the

nonchalant use of casual cruelty. Having suffered from the pain of the cane makes it easier to inflict it on the lesser breeds without the law. Boys in the upper forms were permitted and even assigned to cane the younger boys. They could demand demeaning services and even, it has been hinted, sexual access. This, combined with services from a swarm of menials and a monocultural tradition, made English upper class schools what George Orwell described as a "warm bath of snobbery." Having run the gauntlet, taught that they alone were fit to rule the world, their Colonel Blimps spread their enlightenment across the globe. They have left us a heritage of great literature written, much of it, by rebels who hated the system and fled if they possibly could. And they have left us two gruesome ghosts: A language that cannot be spelled and a cowardly habit of beating upon young bodies, both counterproductive, a pair of albatrosses haunting the halls of learning and impeding progress in a world that needs free roving brains more than mindlessly obedient robots.

Habits are hard to eradicate, social habits no less than personal ones. The erstwhile slaves, children of the dispossessed imbibed the customs and manners of their masters, but having no armies to command, turn on their children to shape them as they were shaped. Thus when members of an American minority say - and feel in their bones - that spanking is a part of their cultural heritage, they are quite right, but it is the English part of themselves, not the African or Native American or Asian part, and the ugliest aspect of the Englishness that they are feeling. Greer and Cobbs pinpointed the source with complete accuracy: It is the tradition of slavery, peonage, of bondage that insists upon the use of physical force in rearing the young.

It is no accident that the two cities that welcomed the Southern Blacks and gave them the most room to grow and develop their human potential have been Chicago and Washington, D.C. In spite of real difficulties these are the centers of Afro-American culture at its best. Black wealth, Black professionalism, Black success is stronger and more viable in these cities than in Detroit or Harlem. Ebony is not published in New York as one might expect; it flourishes from Chicago. Detroit boils with Black crime; Harlem is the symbol of all that's wrong with slum life, the natural setting for "Blackboard Jungle" and "West Side Story" where violence surprises no one. Why the difference? Chicago was home to Richard Wright and a bevy of Black writers and playwrights, and in the nation's capital, corporal punishment is not only illegal, it doesn't happen. In New York until recently, the law against it was broken with impunity; in Detroit, it is not only permitted, but encouraged. In these cities minority success is definitely harder to achieve.

In the end, it just might be racism that will put an end to spanking in schools. There is a special distaste about permitting one's child to be upended by a male of another race. The abject belief that the school knows best is no longer a matter of faith. A hands off policy is far the most likely to succeed.

CHAPTER SEVEN

RELIGION

"Whoso shall offend one of these little ones,
it were better for him that a millstone were
hanged about his neck and that he were drowned in
the depth of the sea." Math. 18:6.

When the Reverend Eugene Yingling and the Reverend
Roger Voegtlin were acquitted of the charge of
conspiracy in the paddling of three year old Jeffrey
Klein, the spectators in the courtroom, members of the
Fairhaven Fundamentalist congregation, stood up and
shouted, "Praise the Lord!"
    The Fairhaven Christian Academy had been in
trouble with the law before. One of their older
students ran away and refused to take any more
beatings. His probation officer agreed to let him live
with a relative and attend another school. The
Reverends Yingling and Voegtlin charged kidnapping and
demanded that the boy be returned to them. Thus, when
they were charged with conspiracy to commit harm to
Baby Jeffrey, they called the county officials
"vultures" who wanted to shut down the school and
persecute them. But now they were vindicated, at least
in part. The battery charge was still to be tried.
    "It is impossible to have a good school without
discipline and paddling is the best and only way to
enforce it," they said.
    "Amen! Praise the Lord!"
    "Children are born depraved; they're born liars.
They have to be trained to do good.... The Bible
teaches that if you love your son, you'll spank him,"
they said.
    "Amen! Praise the Lord!"
    The doctrine of original sin - that people are
born bad - was the subject of centuries of debate by
the Christian Fathers and by the Rabbis before them.
The debates ranged back and forth about free will,
about whether Adam's sin was inherited by all humans or
whether we just imitated him. Most seemed to agree

69

that the wages of sin is death, but they stumbled about
trying to figure out how anyone could be without sin.
The older Fathers taught that every sin is an act of
free will and, consequently, an infant is as incapable
of committing a sin as he is unable to do any good.
But medieval theologians couldn't let it go at that.
Augustine wrote that corruption consists of domination
of lower sensual instincts over the spirit. This makes
it impossible for a man to escape sin by his own
power. Sin and, therefore, death is hereditary.
Thomas Aquinas wrote that sin was disobedience to God
due to the fall of Adam and that an unbaptized infant
is damned. But Duns Scotus believed that sin was
freely chosen. What is one to make of all this?

In hunting through three encyclopedias of religion
to find the origin of the belief that children are born
depraved, I learned only two irrelevant facts before I
dissolved in yawns. One was that there is no reference
to the "Fall of Adam" in the Old Testament, and the
other was that Jonathon Edwards, the same who made the
two hour oration at Gettysburg before President Lincoln
was asked to say a few words, was the author of The
Great Doctrine of Original Sin Defended. I decided I
wouldn't read it. "With malice toward none, with
charity for all...." was obviously a high ethic and
besides it was shorter and much easier to understand.

There is no use telling people like those in the
Indiana congregation who shouted Praise the Lord that
they cannot find Spare the rod and spoil the child in
the Bible. The nearest in meaning is:

"He who spareth the rod hateth his son, but
he who loveth him is diligent to discipline him."
Proverbs 13:24; And,

"Withhold not correction from the child for
if thou beatest him with the rod, he will not
die." Proverbs 23:13.

Those verses, taken as commandments, would seem to
justify paddling. "Reading" the Bible, however, is
more often than not a matter of quoting a verse or two
from secondary sources. Such selective reading can
find justification for almost any activity.
Consecutive reading of the whole of the Book of
Proverbs reveals that we, as a more enlightened people,
have written and enforced many laws forbidding
activities that are recommended in Proverbs.

"The mouth of the just bringeth forth wisdom,
but the froward tongue shall be cut out."
Proverbs 10:31.

A "froward tongue" is a sassy child or, as others
might hear it, a child who speaks up whether to
question or to explain to adults. In neither case do

70

we cut out tongues anymore, although at one time that was a fairly common punishment.

As in Biblical times, we don't like to be made fun of particularly by a gang of rowdy children, but we do not toss them to the wild animals as Ellisha did.

"There came forth little children out of the city, and mocked him and said unto him, ,Go up, thou bald head; go up thou bald head.' And he turned back and looked on them and cursed them. And there came forth two she-bears out of the wood and tore forty and two of them."

What should be the role of the wife if her husband is attacked? If we look to the Old Testament for instruction, we find:

"When men strive together, one with another, and the wife of one draweth near for to deliver her husband out of the hand of him that smiteth him, and putteth forth her hand and taketh him by the secrets: Then shalt thou cut off her hand." Deut. 25:11-12

The rough justice of another age does not constitute a commandment for modern Americans. The pecking of vulturous birds is punishment only in horror films, not in reality. Delinquents are subjected to excessive punishments but blinding by birds is not among them.

"The eye that mocketh at his father and despiseth to obey his mother, the ravens of the valley shall pick it out and the young eagles shall eat it." Proverbs 30:17

Robery Myers, Priest of the Church of Latter Day Saints, Reformed, writes in the Saints Herald:

There are those who contend that because corporal punishment was widely used for adults in Bible times, such discipline should be approved today. It is interesting to note that the same people do not ride donkeys, yet this mode of travel was "good enough" for Christ.

There is always the danger of a man with good intentions taking a Bible verse too literally or out of context, with potentially disastrous results. For example a passage in Mark promises "They shall take up serpents; and if they drink any deadly thing, it shall not hurt them." (But those who took this as a command and established snake handling cults have died from poisonous bites.)

It would seem wise to examine scriptural accounts closely to determine not only what was happening but also how much of the action was the result of a specific command from God. Nowhere

71

does God command men to beat one another.

The command to beat children (if this is the correct interpretation), is as outdated as the command to stone to death unruly children.

If a man have a stubborn and rebellious son, which will not obey the voice of his father, or the voice of his mother, and that, when they have chastened him, will not hearken unto them: Then shall his father and mother lay hold on him, and bring him out unto the elders of his city, and unto the gate of his place.

And they shall say unto the elders of his city, "This our son is stubborn and rebellious; he will not obey our voice; he is a glutton and a drunkard."

And all the men of the city shall stone him with stones, that he die: so shalt thou put evil away from among you; and all Israel shall hear, and fear. Deut. 21:18-21

It is noteworthy that the New Testament, the Book of Mormon, and the Doctrine and Covenants are silent on the subject of corporal punishment for children. In such a case, it would seem that the church is on its own to make a wise decision after seeking wisdom from the best sources....

In an "I Protest" article in the Christian Herald, Edna Mills, R.N., took the Protestant ministry to task for authenticating cruelty to children:

In these days when mankind struggles to find a way out of the present chaos of war between nations, and violence and crime on our city streets, why do so many Christian leaders preach and teach by word and example that 'in the home' violence is right?

A much admired minister and writer of inspirational books has sanctioned the use of corporal discipline, as has also a famous world evangelist.

A minister in a 'Father's Day' sermon, admonished parents somewhat as follows: "To teach obedience and respect, you may sometimes find it necessary to spank your child's bottom.!"

A minister's wife, in speaking to me of a saucy, seven-year-old, remarked, "Someone should take her in hand and slap her up - and good."

A Sunday school teacher has wondered why anyone should slap a child's face when "God has provided a special place for that purpose."

Then, too, I've heard comments such as these from parents who spanked "only in desperation" and

72

felt "not quite right about it," but "our minister spanks his children" and "our minister believes in it" and "our minister says it is all right as long as we punish only in love, never in anger."

Frankly, while I sympathize with an overburdened parent who impulsively and _angrily_ strikes out at an aggravating youngster, and it is tragic that so many parents live under conditions of poverty, ill health, overwork, that lead them either to the frustrating use of violence or to no discipline at all. Yet, I vehemently disagree with those emissaries of life and love who imply that corporal punishment is Christian and healthy. Since more parents listen to ministers than to child specialist, I _protest_ this assumption.

As a nurse, I've been taught to favor procedures which are conducive and oppose those which are detrimental to health and growth, and I am in complete agreement with this statement by the famous Dr. Harry Emerson Fosdick, writer and Minister Emeritus of the Riverside Church of New York: "We cannot make living things grow with a sledge hammer, no matter how hard we pound."

In my estimation, and I'm convinced that most child specialists agree, corporal discipline is a _hinderance_ to total health and mature development, thus, constitutes an abuse and is evil. I believe that the guilt experienced by those parents uncomfortable about its use is a natural response to error, but has too often been stilled by listening to those golden-voiced prophets and clanging cymbals who say, "Parents, let's build more woodsheds and get back to the seat of the problem."

One spends years learning to be a doctor, teacher, minister, scientist. No one just happens to be one of these; yet, all too often, the most important career of all, _parenthood_, does just happen. It is blundered through with little or no preparation. Until, or unless, this situation is legally remedied, I suggest we take time to listen to the man of God who spoke nearly 2000 years ago:
"...As you did it to one of the least of these my brethren, you did it to me." Matt. 25:40
Listen, too, to a writer of that same era:
"There is no fear in love, but perfect love casts out fear. For fear has to do with punishment, and he who fears is not perfected in love." 1st John 4:18

73

I am completely bewildered by the attempt to reconcile violent attacks applied to a child's body as being in harmony with the teachings of Christianity. I ask Christian parents: How could you feel if Jesus unexpected entered your woodshed as you were self-righteously applying the 'rod' to your child? If think He might take the stick away from you saying: "You have a fine way of rejecting the commandment of God in order to keep your tradition!" Mark 7:9. That old 'spare the rod' dogma has too long blurred the conscience of Mankind. Childhood is desperately in need of seeing and <u>feeling</u> Christianity practiced. "And they shall beat their swords into plowshares." Lift not your hand against children anymore.

The First Amendment to the American Constitution forbids Congress to make laws respecting an establishment of religion or prohibiting the free exercise thereof. This has been a blessed heritage. We have never had a religious war although the Bible has been quoted on both sides of many controversies. The Prohibitionists quoted "Wine is a mocker; strong drink is raging..." (Pro. 20:1) and their opponents cited the miracle at Cana. Slavery was defended and attacked with bible verses. Anesthesia in childbirth was finally permitted because "God caused Adam to fall into a deep sleep" before the rib was excised. The somewhat frantic recourse to various verses in Proverbs to defend child abuse is equally useless.

The "free exercise thereof" has limits. To label an action religion does not automatically exempt it from secular laws. The Reverent Liston Pack, pastor of the Holiness Church of God in Jesus Name in rural Tennessee devoutly believed in the Gospel according to Mar, Chapter 16, Verse 18: "They shall take up serpents; and if they drink any deadly thing it shall not hurt them; they shall lay hands on the sick, and they shall recover." His little congregation sought to test the good will of God; two members drank strychnine and died. Tennessee's highest court said the state's need to protect the health of its citizens outweighed the rights of church members to worship in a dangerous fashion. The United States Supreme Court unanimously turned down an appeal by Pastor Pack; his fine and jail sentence stood.

A congregation in North Philadelphia based their devotions on the verse in Proverbs that says that the rod of correction will drive foolishness from the heart of a child. It says nothing about how old is that child, nor of what the foolishness might consist. The spiritual leader, knows to his followers as "Our Father" thought he knew. He attempted to teach four-year-old Jawara Chainey to read but foolishness in the heart of the child prevented. The remedy had been ordained by God, according to scriptures and the rod was applied. He called it "taps" with a belt, and one and then more were given for each incorrect spelling, each mispronounced word, each attempt to withdraw from the lesson. When the police responded to the call of neighbors who heard the screams, they found the child stretched out on the sofa fully clothed, but saturated with the smell of vomit. There were no signs of life. When the police officer went out to his patrol car radio for an ambulance, he returned to the church school room to find the Reverend "Our Father" beating on the dead body. The charge was murder.

The free exercise of religion had limits. Child sacrifice, once a religious duty, is not covered by the First Amendment of the Constitution.

*   *   *   *

The stories in the Bible are better than inkblots to reveal character and attitudes. How, for example, shall we interpret the story of Abraham and Isaac, the Akedah, the trial?

When I went to Sunday School, all the stories had the same moral. Our elders had a single prescription for children and every tale was simplified to illustrate the same these. It was obedience. Adam and Eve were exiled because they were disobedient. Daniel was safe in the lion's den because he obeyed; Jonah obeyed, Paul obeyed. On the final judgment day, people would be divided between those who obeyed and those who did not.

This was convenient for the caretakers and revealed their intense preoccupation with maintaining control, but it shut out the rich heritage of history and human nature as it has been interpreted and reinterpreted down through the ages. Reduced to the obedience theme, the moral of the Akedah seems rather thin: Obey even in a distasteful task and then, if you are willing, you don't have to do it after all. In the light of cultural anthropology, it could be that the story enriches our understanding because it epitomized the end of human sacrifice. The Greeks had such stories too.

During famine, the oracle of Delphi decreed that God would relent if human sacrifice were offered Him. Leos, son of Orpheus, took three daughters and sacrificed them to bring salvation to the people. The

75

famine was checked; the maids of Leos were honored as models of love and fatherland. Aramemnon did not forbear to sacrifice his daughter. Iphigenia, but the Goddess Artemis took pity and substituted a deer of the forest for the girl who was carried off to become a priestess. Pelopidas was promised victory in a dream if he would offer up a virgin with auburn hair as a sacrifice. As he hesitated, behold a mare broke from the pasturing herds, headed in leaps and bounds straight for his tent, its fiery mane flying. Theocritus, the seer, addressed the general: "Here is your victory, O warrior. Heaven has appointed this to be your sacrifice."

Akedah, a theme central to Judaism and Christianity, is endlessly retold and never grows dull; the story rises almost spontaneously in the mind of each generation, says Rabbi Shalom Spiegel. In the early stages of this development, much merit accrued to the parent who was willing to sacrifice his child, and greater merit continued to cling to the completed sacrifice. During the middle ages, Jews were taunted that their father Abraham chickened out on sacrificing his son, whereas the Christian God had completed the sacrifice of his only begotten son; the deed on Golgatha was greater than that on Mt. Moriah. So much shame did this bring down on the beleaguered Jews that Rabbinical lore records many reworked versions in which Abraham actually did kill Isaac who was then revived by angelic dew. In another, Abraham killed Isaac, not once, but twice, his ashes being reformed into a living child by the grace of Heaven. Later, during the 18th Century, Rabbinical studies discovered two distinct religious layers, one from the stratum of ancient idolatry where the sacrifice of the first born was practiced and the other supplied by a more enlightened age which put an end to this cruel punishment. Traces of an editor also remained; some scholar who tried to reconcile the two versions but did not quite succeed. Merit continued to accrue to those who sacrificed. And there still clings to the act of beating a child, an aura of sanctimonious righteousness. It is a gut reaction of ancient lineage.

But interpretations and reinterpretations continue as the world and society changes. Each age has its own needs and circumstances and these affect the story and how it is used. Thus there is precedent for interpreting the story once more to fit ours, the post industrial age. For us, the climactic point and the moral to be learned is the Angel's call to Abraham: "Do not lay your hand on the lad or do anything to him." Gen. 22:12.

Without this understanding we thoughtlessly approve cruelty as the standard child rearing practice. Our disgraceful record of infanticide, battering and brain damaging of children by overpunishment is the result. We are now spending a certain amount of money and effort to rescue child victims and counsel abusive parents. We are not always successful. Particularly difficult are the families in which an unwanted, often secretly illegitimate first born whose presence is gall and wormwood because it acts as a constant reminder of the sin for which the mother cannot forgive herself. Outwardly the brutality to the child is couched in terms of punishment for fault and a sincere effort to do the right thing by straightening him out. Generally the neighbors approve and label the child "neighborhood pest," to which it is but one small step to scapegoat. The villain is not the child; nor is it solely the guilt-ridden parents. The true villian is us, and our American consensus that belting is the royal road to righteousness. What shall we do?

Two men were fishing just below the bend of a beautiful mountain stream. A drowning child, swept by the current, spun into their idyllic spot. Horrified, they dove in, pulled him out, dried him off and gave him food and blanketed him with comfort. It felt good and they smiled at each other. But another cry for help came from the river. Startled, they rescued a second child, then a third. Finally one of the fishermen threw down his rod and began to climb the steep path upstream.

"Hey, where are you going?" his partner shouted.

"I'm going to find out who's tossing all these kids into the river."

Religion is doing as well as believing. Religion takes responsibility for more than the salvation of one's own soul and becomes its brother's keeper and carer. "Be ye doers of the Word and not hearers only." Jesus commanded his followers. Great men, some of them unsung, have dedicated their lives to the doing of the word and thus have subtly steered humanity with small steps and large toward ever high standards of decency. One of these was a Sephardic Jew whose family settled in New Amsterdam in the 1660's. As told by Birmingham in The Grandees, it is the authentic story of how it was that the American Navy abolished flogging three decades before the British were forced to cease that vicious practice after a series of mutinies. Perhaps we can learn from him how a determined humanitarian can abolish flogging of school children.

It was aboard the United States late in the year 1817 that the newly commissioned naval officer, Uriah

Phillips Levy, was required to witness his first flogging. The practice was commonplace. Flogging was advocated as the most practical way to maintain discipline on shipboard. When sailors stripped to the waist for work, it was not remarkable to see that the backs of many were solidly ridged and bubbled with scar tissue.

Flogging was prescribed for such misdeeds as drunkenness, profanity and For Unlawful Carnal Knowledge, the acronym which has become the most controversial of the four letter words. It could be ordered for such minor offenses as spitting on the deck or looking sullen. Needless to say, some Captains were sadistic.

On this occasion, a middle aged gunner's mate had come back from shore leave drunk and had been noisy and abusive. Thirty lashes had been ordered, a relative moderate sentence. Uriah saw how, over the centuries, flogging had been perfected to the point where it was almost an art form of its own. The first few blows softened the muscles of the back. The fourth or fifth blow broke the skin. Then an expert with the lash could direct his blows so that they fell in a symmetrical crisscross pattern, so that the flesh of the back was cut in equal diamond shaped pieces. An alternate stood by in case the first man wielding the whip grew tired. Also, several extra cats were provided so that when one of them grew too slippery from blood to be gripped, another could be substituted.

Men had been knows to remain standing through as many as sixty strokes of the lash, but the gunner's mate, not young, fainted several times during his ordeal and was unconscious when it was over. He was at last cut down from the rack where he had been tied, spread eagle, and pails of salt water were poured over his raw bleeding flesh.

Uriah, sickened by the hideous spectacle, nonetheless forced himself to watch it, never once diverting his eyes. For weeks he could talk of nothing else but the brutality of flogging as a punishment. It was whispered that Uriah Levy disapproved of Navy discipline; there was something subversive about him.

Some twenty years later, after having been cashiered out of the Navy for not getting along with his fellow officers, but having made a fortune in New York real estate and having bought and refurbished Monticello, the home of his hero, Thomas Jefferson, Uriah Levy was restored to his rank in the Navy, indeed promoted by President Andrew Jackson, to Commander. His vessel, however, was a decrepit joke with a rotting hull riddled with rats and a crew that was even sorrier, composed of the ragtag and bobtail of the Navy - drunkards, thieves and misfits of every variety. The incorrigible of every command had filtered down to the Vandalia. He rounded up most of the crew from the town saloons and set about refurbishing the ship including a most un-Navy detail. The guns were gaily painted a bright blue.

His men held him in a curious kind of awe. The first day at sea he announced that he was making a few innovations in regard to disciplinary methods. There would, for example, be no flogging. To his junior officers, this was an astounding announcement. How could discipline possibly be carried out, they wanted to know, without the treat of the cat, particularly with a crew that contained the dregs of naval service? "Have you lost your reason? Flogging is a Navy tradition! This is an open invitation to mutiny!" The Uriah held firm.

Drunkenness and petty thievery were diseases endemic to the Navy, and Uriah devised unique punishments for these offenses. A man found guilty of stealing would have hung from his neck a wooden sign painted with the word "Thief." A sailor found drunk on duty would wear a sign in the shape of a bottle marked, "A Drunkard's Punishment." His lieutenant pronounced these measures not only as futile but ridiculous. But, after a few weeks at sea, an odd fact had to be admitted; they seemed to be working.

Uriah's theory was that to make a man look absurd in the eyes of his companions had a much more lasting effect on his behavior that to torture him physically. And he was an early endorser of the notion that punishment ought to fit the crime. Sometimes this required a bit of creative imagination. One day, an officer brought a young sailor to Uriah. The sailor was accused of imitating the officer's voice, the offense was mocking. Uriah considered the charge, then ordered a few handfuls of seagull's feathers to be collected. When the feathers arrived, Uriah ordered the sailor to drop his trousers. A small dab of tar was applied to each buttock; the feathers were then affixed and the culprit was told to stand on deck for five minutes to the hilarious amusement of the crew. "If you are going to act like a parrot, you should look like one," Uriah said.

At the end of the voyage, he was again relived of his command. This time the court marshal accused him of cruel and scandalous conduct. Seldom in American history have a sailor's buttocks received so much and such intensive scrutiny from men in the highest ranks of the government including the president. The youth, the prosecution claimed, had been permanently traumatized from the humiliating treatment he had received. The court wrote: "We cannot imagine any punishment more degrading. It involved not only the indecent exposure of the person of the boy, but ignominy which should be reserved for the most disgraceful of offenses. The punishment was not only unusual, but unlawful and exceedingly cruel. Flogging would have been more merciful."

But the sentence was mitigated by President Tyler who wrote: "As a substitute for twelve stripes of the cat, the badge of disgrace was worn for a few minutes but no harm was done to the person, no blood was made to flow..." It is just possible that a judiciously placed campaign contribution had a certain effect.

While waiting for his next ship, Uriah took up an extremely subversive activity. He began writing letters to the editor of newspapers in New York, Philadelphia and Washington and in bombastic prose called flogging "antiquated, barbarious, medieval." He cried, "America shall not be scourged!" Soon, he took to the lecture platform and with his crusade and his vivid descriptions of men being lashed held audiences in shocked fascination. Congress reacted. Pro and anti-flogging factions developed. The Navy became even more deeply entrenched in its position and announced: "It would be utterly impractical to have an efficient Navy without this form of punishment."

In 1850, Senator John P. Hale of New Hampshire, attached an anti-flogging rider to the Naval Appropriations Bill. Once again the Navy struck back and again Uriah was stricken from the rolls. At the age of sixty-three, one would think he would give up, enjoy is new young wife, his real estate fortune, and his homes in Monticello and in New York. But no. Uriah was to be vindicated by the array of 75 character witnesses of wealthy and famous people and politicians; the trial ending in a three-day speech by Uriah himself. He was restored to active service. In 1860, he was placed in command of the entire Mediterranean fleet, elevated to the rank of Commodore but died before he could win the Civil War single handed. Nevertheless, it must be remarked that the American Navy acquitted itself rather better in that conflict that the English Navy which waited another mutiny-filled twenty years to the 1880's before similarly abolishing flogging.

The story of Abraham and Isaac illustrates that gentleness succeeds brutality as an historical necessity. As conditions on living become less harsh, humans become less harsh in their dealings with one another. As childhood becomes safer from diseases, starvation, competition from too many siblings and crippling accidents, more people will grow up less traumatized, more nearly whole persons able to realize more of their potential, and, they, in turn, will provide their children with a still more benign surrounding. This has already happened in selected segments of the population. To extend it to all, we need to progress in the direction of human control over nature including our own nature with its heavy load of primordial cruelties. We must forget what people "deserve" and concentrate on what will be the end result for society.

As both contributing cause and result of such a utopian era, we must abolish the lingering customs of a harsher age. Slavery was maintained with the lash. Indeed, the old shibboleth, spare the rod and spoil the child, could easily be read from the original Hebrew as spare the rod and spoil the slave. Robot-like, unthinking, unquestioning, obedience can be beaten into a submerged population, but modern America has too few jobs for the resulting unskilled.

Violence abrogates the need for establishing true, inner discipline in children. Hanna Arendt, in her essay On Violence, suggests the restoration of the meaning of authority. As an authority on the subject, she writes: "Its hallmark is unquestioned recognition by those who are asked to obey; neither coercion nor persuasion is needed." She adds, "A father can lose his authority either by beating his child or by starting to argue with him; that is either by behaving like a tyrant or by treating him as an equal. To remain in authority requires respect for the person or the office. The greatest enemy of authority, therefore, is contempt. And the surest way to undermine it is laughter."

Love and laughter as elements of religion appeal to the confident and the secure. Fear and punishment must be relegated to the dustbin of history.

CHAPTER EIGHT

VIOLENCE AND VANDALISM

Violence against teachers and vandalism of school property are often cited as the major problem in education. The subject rates headlines at least once a year and usually twice. A new incident of violence is not necessary; a speech, a survey, any ringing denunciation by a public figure is picked up by the wire services to spread again the specious warning that young people are dangerous. In 1975 the headlines were particularly startling:

SCHOOL VIOLENCE - LIKE A WAR ZONE

The stories were still more shocking:

The ledger of violence confronting our schools reads like a casualty list from a war zone or a vice squad annual report... The number of American students who died in combat zones of our nations schools between 1970 and 1973 exceeds the number of American soldiers killed in combat throughout the first three years of the Viet Nam conflict.

This was elaborated in great and horrendous detail in newspapers across the country. Local editorials in varying degrees of indignation decried permissiveness and the "rising tide of juvenile delinquency." Some added a cartoon depicting an old fashioned woodshed in use.

These particular inflammatory statements were generated by then Senator Birch Bayh of Indiana to open the hearings of the subcommittee on Juvenile crime in the Senate Committee on the Judiciary. He called in as witnesses a number of superintendents of large city school districts, representatives of school security directors, high school principals and others involved with students. His staff conducted a survey by mailing questionnaires to 757 school districts, of which 68% were returned and received reports from teachers and other individuals who were concerned and wished to

82

contribute their experiences and opinions. Newspapers were scoured for incidents of school crime, most of them written in exaggerated rhetoric with the three R's translated as: Robbing, Rumbling and Rampaging.

A preliminary report was issued titled: "Our Nation's Schools - A Report Card; 'A' in School Violence and Vandalism." This was followed by a more sober official report calmly called "School Violence and Vandalism: Nature and Extent." Source material for hundreds of plots for television series are there: An administrative assistant at Barberton High School near Cleveland was shot and seriously wounded by a seventeen-year-old whom he was repremanding; A shop instructor was clubbed over the head with a mallet in Dallas, Texas on the same day that two fifteen-year-olds were stabbed on their school playgrounds. At Locke High School in Los Angeles, gang warfare broke out during an after school dance in the gym; the fighting spread into the neighborhood and one death resulted. Three times in one semester a teacher was raped on the grounds of a Houston, Texas school, in each case by an intruder who had no business there. In Tampa, Florida, an eight-year-old girl was lured away from the Bay Elementary School and raped in a nearby orange grove. In 1965 there were 13,200 school fires that resulted in damages of $52 million; in 1971 there were 20,500 fires causing $87 million in damages. It was predicted that the next year would easily be over $100 million. In Tacoma, Washington, firebombs ignited a fire that raged out of control at Truman Junior High causing an estimated $260,000 in damage. Six young boys from 6 to 11 set fire to a Deerfield Park Elementary School in Deerfield Beach, Florida. A former student was identified as the one who set fire to the Bowie High School in Irving, Texas. The tales are endless: drugs, prostitution, gang fights, extortion, rape, murder, each one more senseless, apparently, than the one before. Anyone reading the testimony and seeing the pictures of the confiscated weapons: knives, guns, chunkas, razors, switchblades, Saturday Night Specials, bolos, num chucks, chains, and homemade weapons without a name would surely conclude that the schools were indeed as dangerous as a battle ground. It is even possible that "white flight" to the suburbs is due as much to this kind of publicity as to any real distaste for minority children.

What is the truth about all this? What purpose does it serve? What part of the publicity is mere media dramatization? How much of it is political posturing? Do any groups have something to gain by distorting reality like this?

83

For it is exaggerated, distorted and very damaging to children, to the schools and to our American society. On the face of it, how could there possibly have been as many students killed in schools as soldiers were killed in Viet Nam? How many exactly were there? Bayh admitted that the numbers were 11 and 10. Eleven students died in school between 1970 and 1973. Ten American advisers died in Viet Nam between 1964 and 1967 before any troops, conscripted or volunteer, had arrived. How many business executives had heart attacks and died on the golf courses in any three years is not available for comparison. It is safe to say, however, that more children died at the hands of their parents in the safety of their own homes than died in school between 1970 and 1973.

"One of the damaging effects of the mistaken public belief that school crime is escalating at an alarming rate is that the schools are being pushed toward get-tough remedies rather than seeking educational cures." Professor Francis A. J. Ianni and Dr. Elizabeth Reuss-Ianni, both of Columbia University Teachers College were quoted by Fred M. Hechinger in the New York Times: Having made a thorough study, "Their findings and conclusions collide head on, not only with popular perceptions but also with vehement charges by teacher organizations that their members' safety is being ignored by school and civil authorities and that teachers' dignity is diminished by excessive tolerance of outrages committed by students." They also warn that "current responses to reports of school crime and disruption tend to bring back the most negative forms of school discipline."

Not only teacher organizers eager to demonstrate their concern for the welfare of prospective members, but school safety officers' representatives had much to gain. In "The Unruly School" Robert Rubel points out that the unrest on the college campuses filtered down to the secondary schools briefly between 1969 and 1973 but that it had largely subsided in fact while still written about in terms of crime, assault and extortion. "With the implementation of Offices of School Security which had a mandate to keep crime records, many offenses previously disguised as disorders suddenly became crimes. Fights became assaults; trash can fires became arson; broken windows became vandalism or breaking and entering; lost articles became thefts, and so on." In other words, changing the terminology increased the public record of school crime while in fact it was declining and had dropped markedly when the Viet Nam conflict ended. Joseph Grealy, President of the National Association of School Security Directors criticized the Safe Schools Study made by the National Institute of Education because the figures on school crime made by that survey did not include enough "crimes" to persuade Congress to appropriate as much money as he deemed wise. He complained that the Safe Schools Study had used only a random sampling and had selected schools not seriously affected by school crime. Furthermore, said he, offenses to be reported according to the instructions are limited to those reported to the police. "Vandalism, riots, serious tresspass, demonstrations are not included." Most school disturbances can be and are handled by principals but that leaves the necessity for security personnel less obvious.

Appropriations to continue to expand security service depend upon the public perception of school crime as getting more and more out of hand. Their demands for money know almost no bounds. In his testimony for the Bayh committee, Jerry Halvorsen, Associate Superintendent of the Los Angeles Schools, concluding by asking for funds to further train his 300 man security force beyond the training they had from the Sheriff's department. He wanted funds for hardware: intrusion alarms, walkie talkies and personal alarm systems. This last item had been tried in six schools at a cost of $100,000 per school. He wanted them for all the 662 schools at a total cost of well over half a billion dollars for this single item in this single city.

The cost of vandalism includes both the replacement of the destroyed property and the prevention efforts by guards with equipment, but it also included a hidden cost rarely found in official reports. Contractors who replace broken glass have secured those lucrative jobs, as often as not, by playing politics. Kickbacks, padded payrolls and plain theft, are responsible for some of the education money diverted to repair work. According to the Annual Report of Vandalism in Selected Great Cities for 1971-72 by the Office of Research Reports of the Baltimore Public Schools, the cost to replace a broken pane ranges from $1.50 each in Miami to $881 each in Philadelphia. Either the report was carelessly slapped together or no one in Miami had yet discovered the amount of money to be made replacing broken glass in school windows. Looking at the figures in another way, one could conclude that children in Philadelphia actually have a better record. They broke only one window for each 473 pupils in attendance, while children, or someone, in Miami broke a window for each 20 in attendance. New Orleans schools had one broken window pane for each 4 in attendance. When there is money to be made from broken windows, there will be broken windows and no calls for a crackdown on kids will change that.

All this is not to say there is no violence or vandalism. There are no reliable statistics, but before solutions are sought some attempt should be made to separate the damage done by students and that done by others. One serious source of confusion is the lumping together of damage done by students and damage done to students. The Bayh study was particularly remiss in this, but surveys before and since are guilty of the same adding together broken panes and unprotected windows facing a playground and slashed vinyl upholstery on school bus seats with rape of a child enticed away from her school by an adult and theft of equipment that had to be hauled away by a truck. The first probably were done by children; the others could not have been. Arson, similarly, cannot be blamed entirely on children. Few fire setters are caught; those who are caught and convicted are usually highly disturbed individuals long past their school days. A teacher who is robbed and raped in front of her class of third graders or the one who was assaulted in her classroom several hours after school had been dismissed were hardly the victims of students, yet these are all counted as "school crime." Intruders endanger both teachers and students, yet the solutions almost without exceptions concentrate on how best to discipline the students. Some advise a return to more severe discipline; some advise more realistic improvements, but both make the false assumption that "school crime" is committed by students exclusively.

One of the cooler heads at the Bayh hearings was James Harris, then President of the National Education Association. He was aware that all schools are not peaceful learning places "On their face, the available data are alarming." Yet he quoted an opinion poll that found only 3.3% of teachers reported that they had been attacked and 3.2% of teachers said that student violence against other students was a major problem. "However," he added, "no nationwide data on the types of violence, number of students involved etc. are available." His conclusions, far from demanding dollars for pilot projects to supply guards, guns, locks and lock-ups, are an in-depth and thoughtful statement about our present society and our beliefs about it. He lists as causes of school violence depersonalization and the breakdown of the family, alienation of students because of Watergate, the economic situation and Viet Nam; outmoded discipline and unrealistic learning materials and generally inflexibility of the schools themselves, desegregation and public opposition thereto as well as "second generation" integration problems; and lastly violence in society as a whole as a means of settling differences. "No solution to violence in the schools is likely until violence in the nation is brought under control."

Another researcher made much the same findings in a survey in California. Kenneth Washington, Assistant Superintendent of Public Instruction headed a task force charged with finding ways for school districts to identify the causes of violence and to help develop techniques to handle disturbances. He and his staff visited 40 high schools and studied reports from 800 more. Their considered conclusion was that the quality of the administration is a major factor. Other major causes of violence were found to be: uneven disciplinary practices, rubber stamp student governments, oppressive school rules and poor counseling or none at all. Other probable causes included: irrelevance of much of the cirriculum, overcrowding, bigotry and racism in the staff, unconcerned teachers and lastly drugs. He advised that reforms should make school "the most pleasant experience of the student's day."

These criticisms of the schools may have been justified and improvements based on these observations would surely improve the effectiveness of the educational enterprise, but they will not eliminate violence and vandalism. This will have to be a two pronged attack that will take into account that the statistics are inflated for lobbying and recruitment purposes, that normal wear and tear on buildings and equipment is to be expected, that damage and danger due to intruders is a separate and distinct problem not to be reduced by disciplining students and finally that such disorder as is attributable to students can be handled by an intelligent and honest set of behaviors already known and in use.

Protection against intruders is made more difficult by the open architecture and sprawling campuses popular in the sunbelt states. It was made more difficult by the fad, fortunately now passing, for an "open campus" that permitted students to roam at large during non-class periods making it almost impossible to distinguish students from intruders. Entrances to each classroom from out of doors was intended to made the children more "at home" but the informality made centralized surveillance impossible. A sex offender or a psychopath could slip into a classroom of a vulnerable young woman and 25 or so small charges. She could not leave them unprotected and had no way of summoning help. The administrator's office and maintenance staff should be able to monitor unobtrusively all entrances and exits. Parents who wish to visit classes can be asked to stop at the office first to let their presence be known and perhaps be given a pass. It should be possible to keep all doors locked from the outside yet open from the inside so that anyone can exit, but to enter would require coming in through a single monitored doorway. In the high schools, a system of hall monitors can request passes. Loiterers should never be permitted in or near the school buildings. In other words, a school building should be safeguarded with the same diligence and concern for logistics as any commercial enterprise and without any hint that the employees and customers who serve or are served should be punished or harassed or even endure a blanket accusation of incipient criminality.

If I walk into an office building after hours I expect to be stopped and asked my business by an armed guard. I may be asked to sign in and out again when I leave. Doors do not open for each set of offices directly into a parking lot. Such foolhardy arrangements would never be tolerated in the business world. A common sense set of protections should routinely be expected to surround school buildings without bursts of ballyhoo about juvenile crime. The costs for such routine protection should be born by the police budget. It should not come out of the moneys allocated to education, nor should it be headlined as a "surtax on school vandalism" with the implication that childish destructiveness costs more than all the books in the library.

The amount of damage done by adolescents unbloated by amounts attributable to adult intruders is still considerable and definitely needs serious consideration. But there is one more factor that needs to be looked at before we turn to the matter of discipline and how it can reduce trouble. The factor rarely if ever taken into account in discussions of juvenile crime is the matter of apprenticeships. Informal, illegal apprenticeship to a criminal career is a regular feature of slum neighborhood life. Boys do not need to wait until they are sent to prison before learning about crime, although the finer points are said to be acquired there. Their introduction may begin as early as age 6 or 7 when they are offered a nickle to run errands or act as lookout and be continued as they grow a bit by earning a dollar for unlocking a door from the inside after they have been boosted through a broken window or a pried apart screen.

A parent speaking to a commission on school crime that was considering the abolition of corporal punishment in the City of Oakland, California, told what she had seen:

"You talk about kids busting into schools and stealing stuff and I want to tell you they don't do that all by themselves. They can't drive the trucks to carry all that stuff away. They don't even know what to do with it lest somebody buys it from them. I'm telling you how all that stuff gets carried away, all those typewriters and those movie machines and tape recorders and all that heavy stuff. That's expensive you say. Well, I know it is, but don't blame it on the kids. I see them everyday, the recruiters. They drive by real slow. Right by my house and right by the playground and right by the school when its getting out. They see some likely kid around 10 or 12, the younger the better provided the look sharp and they call him over and say real nice, 'Hey kid, you wanna earn a dollar?' and the kid, he don't know no better, he says, 'Maybe, what ya got?' Well they take that kid or more likely 2 or 3 of them and they load them in the cadillac. They always drive one of them big fancy cars. And they take them over in another neighborhood where nobody knows them. They never do a heist right in the kid's neighborhood. That way somebody would spot them and tell the police on them. No. They're smart. They take them across town or somewhere else and they back up a truck and the kids lift the stuff out the window. Sometimes it takes two kids to lift it, it's so heavy. Then they take the kids back to their own - round where they live and give them a dollar apiece. Of course if they get interrupted, the cons, they duck out and leave the kids to get caught. Nobody's very hard on them. The first time they get probation and the cons leave them alone for a while. There are always plenty of kids they can get for a dollar or two. I know this is how they work. I've seen them. My grandson - he's a real good kid, never go in trouble by himself - he's got a record now on account of them no good bums that picked him up. He can spot them easy now. He says to me, 'That's them,' when he sees a fancy car creeping slow-like along the street where the kids are. That's why I'm telling you don't always go blaming the kids when the schools get ripped off. They're too little. Catch the real thieves. Put them in jail. Then maybe they'll leave our kids alone."

To these young Oliver Twists must be added the junior drug merchants. Before the drug pushers on campus are punished for their illicit traffic, we should recognize that all merchandizing is hazardous business and that taking chances are a part of the package. Threats of punishment do not deter a successful salesman, and trainees in the drug business are equally adventurous. Their suppliers take even greater chances and from them the young peddlars learn to shrug it off. It is quite possible that the role models they find on the streets treat them with greater dignity than do their parents and teachers. The same loyalty that accrues to the Scout Master who is friend, mentor and model is accorded the "big shot" who doles our supplies, takes the money and pays the commissions. Control of this traffic is a far greater problem than school administrators can be expected to handle. Expulsion of the peddlars sends them into full time jobs as sales representatives and eventually into the hands of the police or the coroners office to be reported as a drug related crime. Policy relating to control of drugs - and it must be controlled - on school campuses must take the whole picture into consideration. Discipline policy suitable for a school system is totally inadequate when dealing with the end man in an international multi-billion dollar industry.

The remaining amounts of violence and vandalism, probably about 10% or less of what is reported as school crime, does depend upon the kind of discipline meted out in the school and in the homes. Here the suggestion of the perceptive educators, Harris and Washington are wise and where used definitely successful. It is difficult to convince those who experienced much physical punishment as a child and used physical punishment on their children that anything less will accomplish the purpose of preventing wrong doing. The equation: you done wrong = you get punished, has such a long history, traceable back beyond human history, that it is accepted almost without question. Yet all research suggests strongly that the equation does not transpose to: you got punished = you now be good. Not always that is. In individual cases and in the short run it may seem to work out that way, but sociologists who have studied larger groups get other results.

One study in Oregon regarding the relationship of the use of corporal punishment in the schools and school vandalism was completed in 1975, with the result that schools practicing corporal punishment have high rates of vandalism by 3 tc 1. It was a preliminary study comparing schools with similar ethnic and

economic status students enrollments in regard to the
amount and severity of corporal punishment meted out to
the students and the cost of vandalism and theft of
school property.

All schools investigations are suburban/rural
located on the outskirts of Portland, Oregon. None are
poor. The students are white (99%) and live within a
short bus ride of the school. Most (95%) live in
single family dwellings, occupant owned. All the
schools are public, none are crowded, most have
swimming pools, tennis courts and are landscaped in
beautiful settings.

Interviews were conducted during the year February
1974 to February 1975 in twelve school districts
serving approximately 18,000 children, from
kindergarten through twelfth grade, very close to 4% of
the total student population of Oregon. Students were
questioned near the schools, in lunch stores, parks,
etc., except not on school property. Each report of
corporal punishment was triple checked and confirmed by
witnesses and by parents if the students gave such
permission. Questioning was thorough and each school
was called for a confirmation of policy regarding
corporal punishment by the principal.

The vandalism cost was secured from insurance
companies and by direct calls to schools.
Investigators were: Lee Hardy and Virginia Miller,
both of whom had students who attend one or another of
these schools and who first became aware of the
corporal punishment when their children came home
bruised.

School District	Level	Enrollment	Corporal Punishment	Vandalism per Pupil
Redland	Kg-6	600	Little or no	None
Bonneville	Kg-6	41	None	None
Damascus	Kg-12	840	None	None
Welches	Kg-6	300	Little or no	None
Bull Run	Kg-6	70	Little or no	$ .02
Reynolds	Kg-12	3701	Routine in lower grades	$ .87
Parkrose	Kg-12	5052	Extreme in lower grades	$ .98
Estacada	Kg-12	3400	Routine	$1.20
Boring	Kg-6	700	Little or no	$1.71
Sandy	Kg-12	2400	Extreme, severe	$2.08
Cottrell	Kg-6	250	Routine	$3.60
Corbett	7-12	230	Extreme, severe	$4.28

The correlation is not perfect, but the trend is

91

unmistakable. Where there is antagonism towards the children as represented by hitting and hurting them for infractions, whether or not this is done for the child's best interests or in the sincere belief that this is the proper way to socialize the little savages, there is anger and retaliation.

The suburbs of Portland can't tell the whole story. There are comparatively free of the turmoil of desegregation, of inner city overcrowding, and poverty. The few drug peddlars are small time and racial antagonism is minimal, certainly not a factor in the minor damage done to the schools. The total damage was less than that found in the high crime areas of the larger cities but the study is suggestive of what will be found when a major study is undertaken.

Of course a lack of physical punishment is not enough; to genuinely reduce student caused vandalism, a positive program must be added. One of the most successful has included attention to all the factors mentioned by Harris and Washington: Irrelevant cirriculum, overcrowding, rubber stamp student government, poor counseling, bigotry, racism, unconcerned teachers, inflexibility, and social factors. With most of these factors turned about and community cooperation secured and held, there was added a clever pay-off: The amount of money spent the previous year to repair damage done by graffiti, broken light bulbs, broken windows, spilled materials, torn up shrubs, carved initials, jammed lockers, splintered doors, and the like was allotted to an inner city high school for the students to administer. During the following year, all money left over after damage had been paid for was at the disposal of the student council. They debated long and hard between a new curtain for the stage, new band instruments, or paint for a mural in the cafeteria. Whatever they chose, there was pride because they had earned it by reducing the cost of vandalism. As an extra bonus it was found that the drug dealers had been driven a full three blocks from campus. At least temporarily.

CHAPTER NINE

ALTERNATIVES

"I've spent my life looking for alternatives to punitive control and arguing in their favor."

B. F. Skinner
Psychology Today
November, 1972

When wildcatters brought in a gusher on his 40 acres, an Oklahoma squatter came into sudden riches and blew it all on a shiny new Cadillac. Illiterate and too elated to listen to instructions, he drove giddily down the road until it ran out of gas. What to do? He knew about mules. He hee'd and he hawed, but it wouldn't go. Enraged, he shouted, he cursed, he kicked, and ever quirt vowels could not budge the stubborn thing.

Finally, with a little help from his friends, he learned that fine machines have to be fed on demand. Grudgingly, against his principles, he provided the essential input. Along with the gas, the attendant gave him a few pointers: Apply the brakes easy; take curves with care and keep both hands on the steering wheel. On his own he learned that going too fast or too slow was dangerous but beyond that he figured it was useless to pamper.

His new knowledge worked for a little while but, nothing being perfect in this imperfect world, there came a time when Caddy misbehaved. Steam blew out of the radiator, unpleasant noises gurgled up from inside the engine and the beautiful wheels jerked to a wrenching stop. This time he wasn't going to be conned into any more lessons in care care. They didn't do any good anyway.

"T'hell with it," he said, and pushed it off the road.

In handling human children, we do ourselves and society a serious disservice if we brush aside all the friendly advice about child maintenance and insist that

93

there is no other way but old fashioned force. Preventive care, planning ahead, some minimal information about what makes them go and how to better them along the road to learning is essential. Yet, the demand for alternatives is almost always for some immediate action to be taken at the moment when the child disobeys.

"Everybody wants to talk about and view discipline in terms of prevention, improvement, reduction of problems, solutions to problems, etc. This is all very nice, but it misses the simple fact that teachers must also look at discipline on a continuing basis and what specifically do you do when an actual discipline problem arises? This is what everybody keeps ignoring and forgetting," said one indignant teacher leader.

"Don't give me any fluff about not being afraid of silence and touching," said another impatient schoolman. "I want to know what you are going to do right then and there when Johnny misbehaves."

This is a little like limiting the conversation with the insurance agent to: "What do I do after the fire breaks out?"

If he takes you seriously, his advice is sound. "Walk, do not run, to the nearest exit." Immediate action is seldom necessary. If it seems so, cool it. Take a deep breath. Count to ten. Stall until your adrenaline level recedes. Then find out what is really wrong.

"But are you going to take time for a grand jury investigation when a kid is racing for the edge of a cliff? Or are you going to take quick and unquestioned action?"

"Any cliffs in your school?"

"You know what I mean! If a two-year-old persists in stepping off the curb after you've explained a dozen times or if a child's life is in danger, are you going to 'walk not run for the nearest exit?'"

If the use of physical force on children were limited to rescuing them from cliffs and curbs, there would be no problem. Grabbing an infant from the fire is not punishment; hitting him afterward to relieve one's tension is. Holding, restraining arms can embrace or strangle, protect or provoke. The quite different feelings and intentions of the rescuer and the rebuker are expressed in the tension of the muscles, the tone of the voice, the rhythm of the motion and similar clues. Even the newborn is astute enough to recognize and react to such signals with contentment or crying. Body language does not lie. Rescue is not punishment. Let's not confuse ourselves.

94

If that stereotypical two-year-old steps off the curb, lift him back and say firmly, "Wait." And smile, confident that he understands.

If he forgets, repeat.

If he forgets and there is genuine danger, you will want to communicate to him the message _dangerous._ Not "naughty." Not "hurt bottom." **DANGER.** The best messenger, as always for a young child, is body language. Let me tell you what happened:

Seven dashed into the street after a ball. Two toddled after him. I heard the screech of brakes and an angry voice cursing: "Why don't these women keep their kids off the street?"

I reached the scene in a bound and dropped onto my knees to clasp an apparently oblivious two. My heart was pounding with fright and gratitude; my breath came in pants; I couldn't say a word. Then after a minute, two began to cry. I was amazed. Why cry? The danger was over. I was not scolding her. It was just a regular hug. That had never made her cry before.

There is nothing occult about a transfer of information without words. Nor is it extrasensory perception. The clues were clear enough. The child felt the fast heartbeat, the trembling. It said fear to her. The association was reinforced, I am sure, by hearing the tale recounted to her father, to her grandmother and again over the phone. In any case, she never forgot. Indeed, for a while she did not want to step off the curb at all, not even when out for a walk and legitimately crossing with a green light. I had to carry her.

Children absorb information by this kind of osmosis from the trusted adults. If the message is obscured or confused by extraneous signals of anger, hurt, long harangues, punishments, various emotions are aroused; among them defiance, distrust, uncertainty, and other negatives. But communication of an emotion shared, whether fear, shame, joy, peace, will imprint forever.

With school age children, the communication of the appropriate emotion will be more verbal and less intimately body language. A boy has climbed onto a roof or some forbidden spot that is possibly dangerous. Or he may be safe enough himself but inspire younger, less capable children to try until someone is hurt. We agree it is necessary to get him down and to convince him and others that there is to be no more stunting. This is, let us say, a "racing toward the cliff" situation and could occur in any school that had not taken preventive measures. Most children are curious, have a streak of daredeviltry and are challenged by any local Mt. Everest because it is there. What shall we do right then on the spot? What is the appropriate emotion we want to convey? What secondary message will we send to the child about himself?

Long ago, when I was just beginning to read for myself, I found a book in the library that I must have reread a hundred times; I have never forgotten "Little Purdy." Little Purdy had climbed onto the second story scaffolding of a house under construction. When her mother saw her, she was teetering far above the ground on an unprotected two by four. A scream would have frightened her, made her lose her balance and send her crashing to the concrete. Mother had a large bunch of keys in her apron pocket. Gently she shook them to catch Little Purdy's attention. The little one smiled down at her mother. Bravely mother smiled back and held out her arms indicating love, protection, desire, acceptance. Nimbly Little Purdy scrambled safely down and ran to her mother for a hug of pride. She got the hug but she also got the message, "I was very frightened for you." She said, "I'm sorry, Mother. I didn't mean to scare you. I'll never go up there again." That, at least, is the way I remember it.

But now we have male actors instead of Little Purdy and her mother; we have a school yard with a roof where overshot basketballs get stuck and we have an awesome audience of the daredevil's peers about to receive a lifelong lesson on how to act like a man in an emergency.

We can dispense with the keys to jangle but in getting the roof topper's attention we can keep a low keyed tone as we call his name. We had better keep the smile of welcome and most important of all we will be wise to communicate the emotion of fearfulness for his safety and pleasure in his return. An arm across the shoulders, a helping lift off the drain pipe will do. If your throat is dry, the message is carried if you say no more than, "Thanks, Tim, for getting the ball. But it is against the rules, you know." Or you can go on about others not so well conditioned who might fall. But if you call him bad, stupid, insolent, disobedient, reckless, or an S.O.B., you van called Columbus, Marco Polo, Walter Raleigh, Ponce de Leon and all the poineers who ever took a chance in dangerous places equally bad, stupid, etc. If you thwack him or insult him, you have done it onto all the heroes who preceded him.

If tempermentally you simply cannot let go without a punishment of some kind, you can lock up the balls during the hours when that section of the grounds is not monitored. You could require that he pay for the pane of glass in the skylight that he stepped through; you could think of several more natural consequences or require a composition on "Ways to keep boys from climbing on the overhand." You might even glean a new idea from him.

This approach, of course, has to be from a position of strength and trust. If it is done with a helpless air or a pitiful plea to "be a nice boy now," you have announced yourself as a wooly bear to be baited. And you will be. But, if your aplomb comes across as total command, you are the stuff that leaders area made of.

The need to subdue subjects before they could be taught used to be an article of faith in our folklore. Colts were broken with whips and spurs, dogs had to be beaten into submission before they could be trusted. But animal trainers no longer use those methods, not since _Black_ _Beauty_, the _Uncle_ _Tom's_ _Cabin_ of liberated horses, exposed the cruelty for what it was. it now proves possible to tame even the jungle cats with petting and gentling and constant loving care. In those days, too, it was believed that people drowning had to be knocked out with a haymaker before they could be protaged to safety. The Red Cross has taught water safety for half a century and finally laid to rest the "knock-em-unconscious-so-they-won't-pull-you-under-too" nonsense.

So much for the child racing for the cliff. The real cause of the teachers distress is the child who disrupts either the class as is claimed or the teachers peace of mind as is oftener the fact. A popular recommendation is "time out" borrowed from basketball and other team sports in which a player - or the child - is sent from the game for a brief period to a quiet place to regain self control and to let heated passions subside. It may be to sit in a corner or stand outside in the hall for a while, or in more enlightened schools, to a special room equipped with expendable things to manipulate and perhaps a counselor to talk to. The resemblance of "time out" to jail is not difficult to detect; attenuated terms of five minutes rather than five years is the popsickle of prison sentences.

Prison was at first a humane alternative to torture. A quiet time in solitary contemplation of his sins from whence he would emerge a changed man was the kindly Quaker substitute for the hideous spectacles of drawing and quartering popular in medieval Europe. So "time out" is a civilized step toward decency and away from battering at disturbed and disturbing children. But regressions into the use of "time out" as a time of fear and frustration as when confinement is too long or in too small a space or stripped of all stimuli is just that: a regression. Used as a sanctuary to let the adrenaline subside, the quiet corner is valuable; used as a prison cell to deprive the child of participation in the life and activities of his peers, it can be destructive.

Suspension, similarly, is an atrophied form of exile. Being sent to Siberia was not always a death sentence; it definitely was a way of ridding the body politic of an irritant. But irritants have a way of being the advance warning signals of a revolution. Thus, it cannot be thought of as THE alternative to corporal punishment.

Said an indignant administrator: "If we can't hit them, we've got to put them out. That way we are denying them an education!"

The indignation is understandable, the defense of physical punishment is not. But he had a point. Suspension without the provision of some other educational opportunity is a cheap dodge. It is solving a school problem by making it a community problem. It it were not unfair to the unfortunate pushouts, one could describe the system of suspensions as emptying chamber pots out the window into a public thoroughfare. The house is rid of an odor but society suffers.

Suspensions and time out procedures, if very temporary and followed up with careful study and conferencing, can be stop-gap measures definitely a humane step above physical poundings, but by no means acceptable alternatives. If the need for relief from disruptions in the classroom escalates, the impulse to throw them out becomes an addiction. At that point, it is past time to reassess the system and see where the planning broke down and why the poor fit.

ON THE SPOT ALTERNATIVES

If a child picks up a rock to throw, take it away from him.

If two are fighting, separate them.

If a knife comes to school, confiscate it.

If something is stolen, require it to be returned.

If a child talks out of turn, transfer him to a more relaxed classroom.

If you spot a drug pusher, call the police.

If a whole class becomes restless, sing together or read stirring poetry in unison.

For tardiness, apply the same sanctions used in church.

If an adolescent gets the giggles, try a glass of water.

If a child calls another an insulting name, ask
him to apologize. If he does not, apologize
for him and file the matter under "To discuss
later."
If a child calls the teacher an insulting name,
grin and go deaf.
If a child shouts racial slurs, sexual expletives,
coprophilous references, laugh first before
you remove him to a quiet place for further
clarification of the semantic inferences of
his outburst.
In other words, if you are a disciplinarian, think
of your role as an expediter, a trouble
shooter, a Mr. Fixit, but not that of a
judge, jailer or jackhammer.

The list is only partly tongue in cheek. It is a
little like trying to explain what to do when your car
goes into a skid as if that were the sum total of
driving lessons. In an emergency, no one remembers
instruction but most experienced drivers turn into a
skid and straighten out unless they are subsconsciously
suicidal. Long term planning, however, seems to merit
more serious consideration since the question, "Well,
what's the alternative?" is asked as often in true
puzzlement as in belligerent antagonism.

The belligerent try to bear trap the advocate of
non-violence by the rhetorical question, which isn't a
request for information; it is a stylized form of
polite disagreement. It is easy to fall into the trap.
An elaborate smorgasbordt of alternatives is met one at
a time with, "I tried that but..." Or, "Yes, but if
that doesn't work, then what?" The result is to push
the protagonist back to the ultimate case, and with the
reluctant admission that "only as a last resort" it may
be necessary to use physical force, the trap is sprung
and the argument lost. The clear distinction between
corporal punishment and restraint is deliberately
muddied and the need to remove a knife from a deranged
and irresponsible infant is labeled as a need for
permission to spank.

Permission granted and the door is flung wide
open. No one ever uses a paddle on a child except as a
last resort even if it is swung fifty times a day.

"You tell 'em once and if they don't do it you
spank 'em as a last resort," explained a dedicated
paddler.

Others show more ingenuity and do have a series of
resorts before the last one; they may explain, scold,
try to shame, threaten, remove privileges, send to
stand out in the hall, give demerits and finally in

total exasperation send to the office to be paddled.
"There does come a time with some of these kids....!"
But agreement, even reluctant, that the paddling
accomplishes what lesser punishments could not is taken
as confirmation of the prejudgment that there is
ultimate moral permission for each on his own without
hindrance to judge what is reasonable, what is a truly
dangerous situation and at what point paddling becomes
appropriate. Therein lies the danger.

The truly puzzled are also reluctant learners.
They, too, defend their customary method of dealing
with the difficult. They point out that such children
are used to whippings. "That's what they get at home
and that's all they understand." The obvious answer is
that the school is an educational institution and our
dedication to teaching the whole child is long
standing. If non-violent methods of dealing with
interpersonal relations is the area of ignorance, then
that is what needs to be taught. If schools are merely
to be pale copies of inadequate homes, there is little
point in the enormous budget and the escalated
standards of training for teachers. The first
necessity for such teaching is the example of effective
relating on the part of the adult examples.

"Modeling," says Albert Bandura, "is more
important than platitudes in determining behavior. The
message is subtly communicated that the (paddling)
adult approves of aggressive behavior."

The truly puzzled may agree but continue to
profess ignorance about what to use as a substitute for
the paddle. "If you can't hit them, how should you
punish them?" The one track mind cannot - will not -
get out of the rut of punishment as the cure-all. If
not one kind of punishment, then another. Lock them in
a dark closet, perhaps; stretch adhesive tape over the
talkative mouths; tie them down into a chair, forty
laps around the track, no lunch, stay in at recess;
write, "I will be a good boy" 500 times. Ultimately
useless except to increase anger and embarrassment and
to decrease the ability to concentrate on learning
tasks because of preoccupation with daydreams of
retaliation.

The wind and the sun had an argument about
which was the stronger. A man down below on the
earth became the test subject by which they would
settle the matter. "Let us determine which of us
is stronger by seeing who can remove his coat."
Agreed. The wind tried first. He blew lustily.
he blew in gusts and blew in swirling drives. The
man grew cold and clutched his coat about himself
even closer. The wind could not blow it off. He

100

gave up. Then the sun tried. He smiled and shone and smiled and shone even warmer. The man looked up at the sky and relaxed. Then he took off his coat. The sun had won.

The dedicated paddler and the invincibly ignorant will need a categorical verboten and carefully structured alternative, supervised at every step in order to change their prevailing atmosphere from windy to warm. It can be done.

One of the currently popular ways to take the first uneasy step away from punitiveness in dealing with children is the recommendation to "Spare the rod; Use behavior mode." A psychologist or other change agent, armed with stop watch, counter and graph paper, with a computer terminal in the background observes. The number of negative verbalizations and actions are totaled up and compared. The children's behaviors, on target and disruptive, are counted and these data are called the "base line," or starting record. The teacher is shown the chart and told to increase the amount of praise and reduce the amount of scolding and punishment. They may be given a pep talk and motto: Catch The Child Being Good. They may be instructed to hand out tokens as rewards for good behavior. Subsequent observation sessions are dutifully entered on the graph that shows disruptive behaviors of children dropping off as the teacher's negatives become less. When this process has gone on for a while, a month or more, and the teacher is beginning to get used to the new and pleasant ways, the psychologists plays a machiavellian trick. For the sake of experimental data he has to go back to base line to make sure that the change in the children was due to the change in the teacher and not in some extraneous influence no one noticed. The teacher is told to go back to her old ways and to watch what happens to the curves. Some teachers sensibly resist; some are relieved because the effort to be complimentary and to count out tokens takes a lot of psychic energy if one is by nature or long habit a critical person. Sure enough. As the teacher's crabbiness rises, so too the antagonism of the children is recorded in the greater frequency of out-of-seat behavior, in playground fights and miscellaneous silliness. This excursion is supposed to convince the teacher that the experiment was scientific. Sometimes it does. Back once more to congeniality as the keynote and rewards as the payoff, and up go the good behaviors. Then the psychologist departs.

No doubt some good comes from these experiments. They prove again and again that the power figure in any

101

situation sets the tone. The morale of any organization from a family to a multinational conglomerate is a reflection of the input from the power elite. And it proves again that the teacher's expectations are usually fulfilled. If he/she expects disruption, there will be all hell to pay. If he/she expects an eager, curious bunch of kids fascinated by information about what happens on the other side of a globe that strangely on one falls off of and why volcanoes go boom and what number comes after the last number of all, then a curious, fascinated classroom will be. But it is also true that there are ways to reach a non-violent classroom without stop watches and little prizes, which many people consider bribes and destructive of intrinsic interest in the subject matter. If a child is concentrating on winning enough tokens so that he/she can exchange them for free time, then free time becomes the prize and knowledge about our world becomes the chore merely gone through without heart. That may be, but it is a step above chaos and two steps above fear, force and pain to maintain an artificial quiet that passes for school room order.

Teacher Effective Training (T.E.T.) is a more sophisticated system. It followed P.E.T. (Parent Effectiveness Training) and has been followed by L.E.T. (Leadership Effectiveness Training) and Y.E.T. (Youth Effectiveness Training), all of which teach communication, primarily as adapted to the needs of the various roles played out in the drama of getting along with people. We send messages, teaches Thomas Gordon, the guru of Effectiveness, loaded with inadvertent feeling tones that increase alienation. We send "you messages." "You are bad." "You did wrong." You must think, feel, do other than what comes naturally. While these statements may be true in one sense or as we see it, they rouse relatiatory anger, shame and denunciatory "you messages" in return. This escalates our own anger and frustration and adds fuel to the flames of controversy and misunderstanding. Instead of this, Effectiveness Training teaches and conducts practice lessons in active listening. Active listening implies hearing, not only the words, but the feelings behind them. "it means feeding back a response both intellectually on target and emotionally in tune." Parents and teachers by the thousands have learned from these comparatively simple techniques that children who are not heard, who cannot made a dent in the thick wall of adult obtuseness, turn in frustration to restless, attention-seeking devices. They cannot hear our instructions if we do not listen to their feelings.

A somewhat more complex model of effective

communication is offered by the disciples of Eric Berne in Transactional Analysis (T.A.). The inclusion of greater self understanding in recognizing that all of us wear different hats on different occasions and not always appropriately makes an interesting analysis of our various selves. Each of us can act like a child, like a parent or like an adult. It a child speaks to us in childish complaint, it ill behooves an adult to answer him as he might another child. But it can be fun to be childlike sometimes as when reading the _Jungle_ _Book_ or _Where_ _Go_ _the_ _Boats_ to a cuddled up four-year-old. If the boss bawls us out like a tyrannical parent, it may or may not be helpful to respond as a dutiful child. If he speaks as one adult to another, a meeting of minds becomes easier. But to speak as an adult, matter of factly, on another occasion may definitely squash a tentative romance. Berne's book, _Games_ _People_ _Play,_ has been a best seller for many years and has been flattered by many imitators. _Games_ _Students_ _Play_ is recommended to high school counselors and administrators if they want to keep a robust sense of humor and if they have mastered enough transactional analysis to recognize readily the games that they themselves play.

Schools _Without_ _Failure_ by William Glasser, M.D., corrects a tendency if it exists, to be too sympathetic to the deviant one thus deepening the feelings of helplessness and inadequacy. Stop feeling sorry for yourselves, kids, says Glasser in effect, and take responsibility for your own life. Pick up whatever hand the world has dealt you and play it the best you can. But this is no return to: _Pick_ _out_ _and_ _Push_ _the_ _fit;_ _Punish_ _and_ _Push_ _out_ _the_ _unfit._ To Glasser, all children are "fit" and can succeed at something.

Adlerian psychology Americanized by Ansbacher and Driekurs in their several books advocate natural consequences rather than corporal punishment which "leads to low courage in adulthood." Letting the punishment fit the crime means restitution rather than expiation. The child must restore or repair what he has taken or broken, but need not suffer additionally. If he has broken a promise, he is not trusted on the next occasion when he asks for a special privilege. There is no element of getting even in this recipe; it is aimed at helping the child toward mature responsibility. Adler also advised adults to avoid power struggles with the young because the young always win in the end even if only because they live longer.

So much for special systems. There are more. A how-to bibliography should overwhelm the wide-eyed wonders who think that alternatives need to be

103

invented. Education libraries have shelvesful and each year's list of new publications adds a few more. Just to add to the clutter here is another idea, this one by an official of a large local of the American Federation of Teachers. He was explaining that some elementary teachers don't understand how to negotiate. "They complain about a bad principal, for example. They want the Union to get that principal OUT! Nothing else counts. They won't consider a compromise. We have to teach the, and sometimes it's hard, that what they really want is some aspect of their working conditions modified. We might, for example, persuade the principal to cease standing in the office each morning checking the time each teacher signs in. In return the teachers will agree to something that he wants."

The best way to learn something is to teach it. The best way for teachers to learn the art of conflict resolution is to teach these very skills beginning in kindergarten and reaching a professional level by Junior High. No social studies lesson is more important. The ability to compromise, to accept half a loaf, to apologize, to learn that "only teasing" is really insulting, to develop past the point where everything is either pure evil or pure good and that we all live in the grey areas - these are among the social lessons that can and should be taught.

Scene: Second grade. Children storming in after recess. Beautiful blonde doll telling the teacher inn all solemnity: "Ricky and Chuck was fighting on recess!" Teacher, also blonde, but thirtyish and not as beautiful as seven; "Oh?"

Crowd of little girls as Greek chorus, "They was! They was!"

Teacher: "Oh?"

Enter gladiators, sweaty and disheveled, followed at a respectful distance by their liege horde.

Teacher: "Ricky, Chuck. Would you come here, please?"

Ricky: "I didn't do nothin'."

Chuck: "He started it!"

Teacher: "Let's discuss it. Sit down everyone. We will have as our social studies topic this afternoon, CONFLICT RESOLUTION." (She prints this on the board.)

"First we have to have the facts. Who would like to tell us what happened?"

"He hit him!"

"He hit me fist!"

"They was fighting!" General and conflicting statements tumbled out in a jumble of soprano voices.

Teacher: "First we must sit down. Then we must

agree on a few ground rules: We will talk one at a time. We will listen to others. We will try to find a solution. This time we are not having a trial to find out who was guilty. We will not have a judge. There will be no punishment."

Gasps of surprise at this last. Visible signs of relaxing of the tension of the two combatants. Whispered disapproval, "When you do bad you gotta be punished." Whispered misunderstanding, "They're gonna get it!"

Teacher: "It is true that there is a school rule against fighting. But this time we are going to try to find other ways." She wrote OTHER WAYS on the board. "Now we will listen to both sides, one at a time. Ricky, will you tell us what the disagreement was about?"

Ricky: "Well, I had this ball, see? And he knocked it out of my hands."

Chuck: "It was not! It was still my turn."

Patiently the teacher drew out from each no only the facts, but the feelings of the combatants and the others who watched and had shouted encouragement, pausing now and again to put new words on the board: MISUNDERSTANDING, COMPROMISE, AGREEMENT. A half hour had gone by and it was time for math.

"We will continue our discussion tomorrow, but for homework I want each of you to think about 'Other Ways.' If you want to talk about it with your family, that will be fine. We want to think of as many other ways to settle a dispute as possible. Other ways, not fighting."

Discussions with second graders are not easy. The impulse of the child to blurt each thought as it flashes is almost irresistible, but orderly talk does become almost possible with practice. The teacher who is fascinated with the possibilities that these children harbor within their budding personhood will enjoy and be rewarded by the increasing order and maturity of the debates. Regardless of the conclusions arrived at, the very fact of having had a more structured consideration of their personal affairs lifts the fracas above the level of replaying the primordial drama and into the age of shuttle diplomacy and Soyuz/Apollo handshakes in space.

However handy one system or another may be for inservice training sessions, the true antidote for behavior that seems to merit discipline is a dynamic curriculum. The plain truth of the matter is that schools where the wood swings freely have the last of interest to offer. The children are bored and the old proverb about what the devil finds for idle hands is still pertinent. The rationalization for the dull and lifeless program is usually that learning is a duty, it's not supposed to be fun and games and that the students simply must get down to work and do the job whether they are interested or not. Life is hard; it includes many dull chores that are essential; why should young people expect life to be a perpetual Disneyland? The grain of truth in this pronouncement is blown up into a whole crop of incredibly busy-work fillers. The child, baffled by pages of nonsense syllables, doodles his time by pattern marking instead of reading and deciding, and, yet, is accounted an acceptable student because "he tries,"and "at least he's quiet." The fact is he is not learning any useful skill, but only how to disappear into the woodwork when the teacher is looking.

Workbooks that consist of endless pages of multiple choice, odd one out and fill in the blank are dreary beyond any mind's imagining. Nothing on the page teaches. It is all testing, testing, testing. If the child knows the right answer, there is no need for the exercise. If he does not know the answer, there is not way to find out. Presumably the teacher is ready to answer questions but she is swamped by 30 clamorous individual questioners and learns in self defense how to put them off.

Individualized instructions may be the major villain. Conceived as an antidote to lockstep lessons in which every child regardless of his abilities or interests was required to do the same lesson at the same time as his 29 (it was 39 or 49 in those days) classmates, individualized learning was to let every child advance at his own pace and follow the dictates of his own drummer. The teacher was to move about answering questions, giving encouragement, redirecting when mistakes occurred and helping each child keep a record of his own progress. Competition and thus losers were to be eliminated. It sounded ideal. No child ever failed. A parent might be told, "Johnny is making good progress at his own speed," when the facts were that Johnny was sitting in a fifth grade classroom still scratching at a second grade phonics book. But he was not failing. Ad the speedster who had finished that second grade phonics book in the spring of his first year in school was supposed to go on to the next book when he returned in the fall for second grade.

It never worked out that way.

When speedy entered second grade, he had a new teacher who did not believe in looking at records; she wanted to make up her own mind about each child. So the whole class started with a review of first grade work and then could again go at their individual pace. Fifth grade Johnny, meanwhile, working in his second grade reading workbook was expected to do his fifth grade social studies homework. It became a nightmare of mixups, repeats, skips, changes and contradictions. it still is. But worse than that, it meant that no two children ever study the same thing at the same time. No one can call up his friend and ask, "What did you get for the fifth problem?" Chatter on the playground can never be on the content of what they are supposed to be learning. No one can propose "Let's play Sir Walter Raleigh!" because the others are reading and comprehending something else. All that conversation can be about is the single common denominator of their lives: television. Or about whose turn it is to have the ball.

Adding to that nightmare are those teachers who rarely correct the workbooks, rarely check individual achievement and who react only to a class, never to a child. Some of these might have been good teachers once, but, beset by contradictory orders from an inept administrator, by too much supervision that is felt as spying or too little supervision that feels like neglect, or whirled abut by new and faddish community proposals changed with each season, they have burned out, given up, go through the paces while the galvanizing principle called "heart" is not in it.

The result is public indignation about children who reach senior high school while still functionally illiterate and stirring calls for proficiency tests to be passed before a diploma is awarded. By then, of course it is too late for the stumblers who have already dropped out.

A combined corrective for the ready use of the paddle either as a first or last resort, and excessive suspensions began gaining popularity in 1979 and 1980. It consists of a sophisticated version of time-out along with attention and tutoring when it turns out that the troublemaker is two or more reading levels below expectation. Most troublemakers do fall into this category but under ordinary circumstances no one discovers this or no one really cares. The solution is a thoughtful and caring version of "in-school suspension." It has proven very popular where tried because the teacher is rid of the disruptive one for a few days; the administrator is given credit for having done something and an extra job is opened for the monitor of the in-school suspension room. Under optimal arrangements it works like this:

A student judged to be in need of correction because of excessive unexcused absences, disruptiveness, or otherwise breaking school rules in such a way that paddling or suspension might otherwise be in order, is assigned to in-school suspension for 1, 2 or 2 days. The room is in the charge of a teacher or counselor and each regular teacher sends assignments that the student is to complete so as to keep up with his class work. He is free to ask the one in charge for help, but he is not permitted to speak to any others serving a similiar sentence. He is not permitted to take part in school activities such as athletics, music, socials, or expeditions. His lunch may be brought to the room and he is dismissed at the regular time. During this time a school counselor or someone acting in this capacity reviews the school record, achievement scores and other data, or schedules a reading test or whatever seems appropriate in each particular case. Difficulties are uncovered if they exist and plans are made for tutoring, an adapted schedule of classes planned if deemed wise. This must be remedial in intent and in fact. Demotion for punitive reasons is never permitted. It it turns out that there are not difficulties and that the disruption was merely high spirits or teasing or on a dare, the student has been punished. If there are not difficulties, a golden opportunity can be seized to turn the slide to disaster into a patch job before it is too late.

There are many advantage: Boys and girls are not turned out onto the street or given carte blanc to sit home and watch soap operas all day. It eliminates the curious custom of rewarding wrong doing by providing vacations. Best of all the big brave ones who would rather be spanked and have it over with are required to face their real problems. They hate it. They call it "jail."

CHAPTER TEN

LAW AND LEGALITIES

Rapid scanning of the Supreme Court decision in 1977 produced a rash of headlines: SUPREME COURT OK'S SPANKING! There followed editorials and columns chortling or bemoaning, but almost all accepting the interpretation of the decision as the final blow to the idea of abolition. They were wrong.

A more recent case in the Federal courts came to a different conclusion. The 1980 news, although it drew fewer headlines, was that when the punishment exceeds the crime, the Constitution does protect children after all. It started in West Virginia.

The Hall family of Roane County has three children: Mervin, Linda and Naomi. They attended the Left Hand Grade School and each in turn was abused by the seventh grade teacher, G. Garrison Tawney. In spite of the parents' repeated requests that their children not be physically abused, Mervin was beaten so badly that he ran home from school. When Linda reached seventh grade she had to be hospitalized from the blows she received and after she recovered was sent to live with relatives to attend another school. Her night terrors promptly cleared up and she had no further trouble. Naomi in her turn was taunted and threatened that she would get what Linda got only worse, but got through her year with Tawney with good grades only to be attacked in her eighth grade year just before Christmas.

According to the legal complaint Naomi was struck across the left hip and thigh with a homemade paddle made of hard, thick rubber from a temporary base used in softball games. In attempting to protect herself she was thrown against a large stationary desk then vehemently grasped by the right arm and twisted into the presence of the principal, Bernard Claywell, who authorized the teacher to strike the 14 year-old girl again. She was beaten repeatedly and violently and was injured so badly that she was admitted to the emergency room of the local hospital. For ten days she was

treated for bruises, broken blood vessels and possible
injuries to the lower back and spine. The hospital
bill (this was 1974) was over $2000. The Hall family
sued.

Attorney Daniel F. Hedges of the Appalachian
Research and Defense Fund of Charleston representing
Naomi and her parents entered suit in Federal Court but
the action was dismissed because in the meantime
Supreme Court had decided - or so it seemed - that
corporal punishment, no matter how severe, was not
unconstitutional. Hedges appealed and in May 1979
arguments were heard by the U.S. Court of Appeals for
the Fourth Circuit. A year later, on May 9, 1980 the
decision was published vindicating Hedges and the Hall
family. To their great joy Appeal Court said in
effect: If all these claims of knocking about and
serious injury and malicious harassment of the older
brother and sister be true, then they have a case which
should have been truly tried, not dismissed. Try
again!

Since I am not a lawyer, I found the legal
twistings and turnings somewhat tough to untangle. It
was a bit like a frustrating trip through an amusement
park fun house, except that it wasn't funny. The maze
of double backs, dead ends and surprise exits in the
published decision is booby trapped with strings of
undecipherables like 395 F. Supp. 294 (M.D.N.C.) (three
judge court) aff'd 423 U.S. 907 (1975), which a lawyer
would recognize at once as the decision in the Baker
case giving teachers the right to spank children over
their parents' objections. Except it says no such
thing. It says: Nothing in the American Constitution
forbids teachers from applying corporal punishment to
children, regardless of their parents' wishes, and that
any rules about such matters will have to be made by
the states or by the people.

With the help of several lawyers, rewrite editors
and other clever people I have finally grasped (if only
at the level of a high school civics class) the fact
that the Supreme Court does not decide whether things
are right or wrong, good or bad, but only whether the
specific reasons given for complaining can be found -
with their own special magnifying glasses - in the
American Constitution and the Amendments thereto. The
newspaper headlines in the Ingraham case, thus were
distortions of the decision which merely said that the
particular reason brought before them was not
applicable.

The Eighth Amendment, the Supreme Court found,
applies only to adjudicated criminals. Even if there
should be confined in the same juvenile institution

110

both criminal and status offenders (muggers and mere
runaways) and the two boys should commit the same fault
(sassing a guard for example) they could be treated
quite differently. The one who had stolen a car and
knocked down an elderly persons could no be whipped;
the neglected and abandoned child who had broken no law
could be.

Furthermore, the Court refused to consider the
matter of severity. It sounded rather pettish but the
major opinion announce that the Court could not be
bothered deciding in every case of school discipline
whether 5 strokes was suitable punishment or 10 strokes
was the proper amount. But the Ingraham boy on whose
behalf the suit was brought had no had an ear cut off.
He had been forcible held down across a table by two
husky adult males and thrashed 20 times. Some reports
have it 50 times. Hospitalization for ten days, he
needed medication for pain, for constipation and for
shock. By any reasonable standard this was excessive
even if his misbehavior had been greater than it was.
He had been slow to move when ordered off the stage.
Annoying, no doubt, but hardly deserving of such a
thrashing. But the Court was not considering justice
at this time. It was considering whether this was a
federal concern or should be left up to the states.
It was shaved even finer than that. It considered only
the Eighth Amendment and whether that was applicable to
school children being disciplined and decided it was
not.

But there are additional reasons. Child advocacy
groups took too pessimistic a view of Ingraham. There
were a number of positive implications in the majority
decision which should have been given more attention.
On page 22 the Justices seem to be telling the lawyers
for the children how they should have pleaded.

"Where school authorities acting under color
of state law, deliberately decide to punish a
child for misconduct by restraining the child and
inflicting appreciable physical pain, we hold that
the Fourteenth Amendment liberty interests are
implicated."

Attorney Hedges for the Hall family took this
advice seriously. In preparing his appeal he ignored
the Eighth and concentrated on the Fourteenth
Amendment. Originally designed to insure the full
rights of citizenship to the newly freed slaves, it has
since been used for a wide variety of other purposes.
Abolishing the thrashing of children by way of a law
designed to protect erstwhile slave, has a certain wry
justice. Here it is with the key words emphasized:
All persons born nor naturalized in the

111

United States, and subject to the jurisdiction thereof, are citizens of the United States and of the State wherein they reside. No State shall make any law which shall abridge the privileges or immunities of citizens of the United States; nor shall any State deprive any person of life, **liberty**, or property, without **due process** of law; nor deny to any person within its jurisdiction the equal protection of the laws.

"Due process" is a concept dear to the hearts of lawyers. It's the way they make their living. They have divided it into two parts: procedural and substantive. The meaning of the first is clear; the accused must have a fair trial. In the case of children it has come to mean the right to a hearing, however informal, with an opportunity to present the child's side of the story. Substantive due process is not as obvious, but it is the point on which Hedges won his appeal, thus it behooves the general public to understand. Briefly, it means that the punishment may not be greater than the minimum necessary to protect the state's interest in keeping order on the school premises. Just as a policeman is permitted to use sufficient force to take a suspect into custody but no more, so a school disciplinarian may use only such force as is necessary to keep order but not more.

A policeman who had a suspect's stomach pumped out - perhaps to find evidence - had overstepped the bounds of substantive due process. The unprovoked beating of a pre-trial detainee by a guard was also held to be unconstitutional. It would seem that beating a child so as to raise welts, break blood vessels and hospitalize her for ten days with possible back injuries must surely be judged greater than was necessary to control, as is now claimed, "vulgar language." Police are trained not to react to vulgar language or even to personal insults; It would seem that teachers may need similiar retraining. Naturally teacher are free to, indeed have the responsibility to, teach acceptable language, but not to react to it with savagery. The Hall v. Tawney judgment stated:

"The existence of the right to ultimate bodily security - the most fundamental aspect of personal privacy - is unmistakably established in our constitutional decisions as an attribute of ordered liberty that is the concern of substantive due process."

Thus teacher brutality is equated with police brutality. Both are expended on non-criminals - people not, or not yet found guilty of a crime - and both are unconstitutional. It is one small step for childkind.

112

The decision is a landmark in that cases may now be tried (which Ingraham seemed to rule out) in Federal Court when there has been injury comparable to police brutality such as, for example, the boy in the Sanford, Florida Middle School who was on an operating table in a Sanford hospital thirty minutes after a paddling because surgery was required for torsion of the tests. The boy with three others had been tossing jelly beans and pebbles at a tool shed on the school grounds. If police had caused that much damage to an adult for so trivial a nuisance, they would be disciplined at once, if Constitutional law is followed.

Damages awarded by Federal Courts are likely to be greater than those awarded by State Courts according to both sets of lawyers in the Hall v. Tawney case. Since state laws and Courts vary this will be a greater advantage for some than for others. In Connecticut a teacher who broke a child's collar bone appealed the decision against him claiming that he was immune from such a suit since he was an agent of the state and acting in that capacity to enforce school rules. The Connecticut State Supreme Court held that he was indeed liable.

"The power to punish... does not include punishment which is disportionate to the offense, unnecessarily degrading or likely to cause serious or permanent harm."

The teacher paid $4,500. But other states might not have so ruled. In many places local courts would have ruled that since the teacher had not planned nor intended to break the boy's bone, he was not guilty. In Sanford the Attorney for the Seminole County State's Attorney's Office said no charges would be filed because there was no evidence that Principal Pelham or Dean of Students Hunt who did the paddling, had acted with malice or had intended to damage the boy. This question, whether unintended injuries leave the teacher liable for damage he has caused will probably be argued in state and local courts many times more and the teachers responsibility to be aware of health and physical conditions debated and, it is hoped, decided.

One additional constitutional point is yet to be considered in corporal punishment cases. "Equal protection of the law" is also guaranteed by the Fourteenth Amendment, but has yet to be argued in regard to corporal punishment. It can be. When just the right case is taken by just the right lawyer and the defendants appeal it to the Supreme Court, these two points of law: substantive due process and equal protection of the law may yet spell the doom of the teachers right to spank.

113

That may not be necessary. If the right case does not get to the Supreme Court and if State Legislatures continue to lag behind the growing desire for reform, it may be that insurance will prove to be the key to abolition. School Boards, teachers organizations and individual educators are taking out policies in great numbers. Many teachers feel that they need the same kind of protection that medical doctors have against malpractice suits, but the policies are not exactly comparable. Teachers usually divide responsibility with principal, superintendents and school boards, and those who belong to unions or associations or professional societies can often call upon these groups for protection and legal expenses. It is not always clear who is liable and who will pay in many cases.

A story out of Baton Rouge, Louisiana may illustrate some of the possible confusion. The page wide headline in the State Times on the day before Christmas, 1980 read: "A KICK IN THE PANTS THAT COST THE SABINE SCHOOL BOARD $2,850."

Principal Green has only two hands. One held a dish, the other a tray, so when he saw two lads about to start a fight, in the cafeteria, he used his foot to get their attention. Kicking 13 year-old Robert Hicks was against Board policy and his mother sued Greene, the School Board and the Board's insurer. The Board disclaimed responsibility because there was "bodily injury" exclusion in its policy. Greene had to hire his own lawyer.

State law in Louisiana, passed in 1975, provides that if a teacher is sued in connection with discipline the school board must provide the teacher with a lawyer and cover the costs of expenses in relation to the case. The law also provided that if the teacher loses and if fined, the board must pay the fine, court costs, etc., unless the court specifically finds that the teacher was malicious and "willfully and deliberately intended to cause bodily harm." But Greene also was covered by his professional association, the Louisiana Association of Educators. Who should pay?

When Robert's mother filed suit for the "embarrassment and humiliation" that he suffered, the school board argued, in effect, that if anybody has to pay anything, it should be the two insurers, that of the board and that of the L.A.E. Greene argued that he shouldn't have to pay anybody anything but if the court decreed otherwise the school board should be the one and they should also pay his lawyer. The district court found Greene guilty, that he should pay $500 to the boy's family and bear his own expenses. He appealed to the Third Circuit Court of Appeal which changed the verdict. It ruled that Robert was not permanently damaged and that the humiliation was no greater being kicked that it would have been with a paddle. The $500 award was reduced to $100. Greene was held not to have been malicious and had not intended bodily harm. Therefore under the 1975 statute the board had to pay the fine, court costs and $2,750 for Greene's lawyer. They could not collect from the teacher's association because the board had no contractual relationship with them and they could not collect from their own insurance company either. The taxpayers paid. The lawyers made a living.

A spokesman for the insurance company that provided coverage for L.A.E. members said that Louisiana has more litigation than any other state in which it writes coverage, and much more litigaition stems from corporal punishment. Many school boards, he added, are adopting rules that discourage or even forbid corporal punishment. In Texas exactly that is happening. Hurst, Texas, embroiled in a civil lawsuit in which a million and a half dollars is being asked, is experimenting with in-school suspension. John Spicer, deputy superintendent gave an additional reason: Because of Title 9, discipline in school should be equal for boys and girls. A gynecologist who sits on the school board insists that because of the physiological make-up of girls they should not be paddled beyond the sixth grade. The school administrators have now talked themselves into agreeing that on-campus suspension is stronger discipline than licks.

*   *   *   *

The original legal justification for spanking children in school was the doctrine of <u>in loco parentis</u> - in place of parents. Although this has no Constitutional or Biblical basis, it is used to justify all manner of knocking about on the theory that that's how parents do it and whoever is acting n place of the parent should have similiar rights. This argument is never used to permit teachers to authorize medical intervention as a parent would; no teacher can order incarceration of a child as "incorrigible;" no teacher is responsible for feeding and clothing and housing a child as parents are. In fact, the single parental activity that is transferred to the teacher is the right to hit. It is a strange anachronism but the thirteen states that have no laws at all about school discipline leave the courts to rely on the English common law - and that includes <u>in loco parentis.</u>

It is worse than strange. It has grown monstrous. Not only may teachers spank as a parent would under this convention, but they may also hit harder than a parent might; they may hit children whose parents never do hit them, and worst of all they may hit even when the parent forbids.

The opinion of the Attorney General's Office, State of Maine will help to clarify, since this doctrine was the primary concern when the Maine legislature abolished corporal punishment. An Inter-Departmental Memorandum dated June 17, 1976 explains:

As a result of enactment of the Maine Criminal Code, effective on May 1, 1976, corporal punishment is no longer a justifiable means of punishing a student although the use of reasonable physical force is recognized as being justifiable means of bringing a disturbance under control or of removing a student who is causing a disturbance.

In Maine, the relationship of teachers to their pupils has been in the nature of "in loco parentis." In an 1847 case the Court noted that parents have the authority to discipline their children as needed and that the parents may delegate that authority to a tutor or an instructor in conjunction with the education of their children.

In an 1886 case the Court held that in the absence of school board guidelines, it was largely within the discretion of the teacher as to what punishment should be imposed in a given situation. The Court further held that the teacher would be held to the "reasonable man" standard as to whether the corporal punishment was excessive:

"'A schoolmaster has the right to inflict reasonable corporal punishment. He must exercise reasonable judgment and discretion, in determining when to punish and to what extent... (T)he teacher is not to be held liable on the ground of the excess of punishment, unless the punishment is clearly excessive, and would be held so in the general judgment of reasonable men.' ...The correct rule holds the teacher liable if he inflicts a punishment which the general judgment of...(reasonable) men, after thought and reflection, would call clearly excessive."

In "in loco parentis" relationships between teachers and their students has thus been recognized at least since 1847. (It is, of course much older. The English Jurist Blackstone who enunciated it in the 18th Century was referring to schooling as it was then. Private tutors were added to the household as soon as Nanny taught the upper class infant to read. For

116

others there were no schools.)

This relationship (in Maine) remained unchanged until the Main Criminal Code became effective on May 1, 1976. Chapter 5 of the Code... deals with specific acts which are justifiable and therefore constitute defenses to what might otherwise be crimes.... The Legislature defines justifiable use of force by a teacher upon a student as being only such "a reasonable degree of force against any such person who creates a disturbance when and to the extent that he reasonably believes it necessary to <u>control</u> the disturbing behavior or to <u>remove</u> a person from the scene of such disturbance."

Corporal touching is therefore justifiable although corporal punishment is not. Corporal punishment of a child may only be imposed by a parent or others who have similiar "long term general care and welfare" responsibilities toward the child...." The legislature contemplated that a teacher is "entrusted with the care and supervision of a person for special and limited purposes only, rather than the long term general care which a parent has for the child."

The end result is that corporal punishment may no longer be inflicted upon a student by a teacher. A teacher who inflicts corporal punishment on a student after May 1, 1976, may no longer assert as a defense in a criminal proceeding that such punishment was justifiable because of the "in loco parentis" relationship between himself and the student.

Other states may well follow Maine's lead.

Maryland's way of abolishing was the easiest but also the least effective. The State Board of Education voted to ban all paddles and other forms of physical punishment. That worked well in the Baltimore to Washington corridor but the farming counties along the water with large rural Black populations sought exemptions from the Legislature and it was granted. The School Board ruling was effectively nullified.

*   *   *   *

What is the best procedure to abolish this ancient evil? It will probably have to be done piecemeal as parents and professionals are convinced that it is not in their best interests, quiet disregarding what is best for children. Any group that decides to accept the challenge will need information first. To list the laws by state is beyond the scope of this book. Laws and regulations are in a state of flux and advocacy groups are best off with current correct information. This can be secured from the Office of the Attorney

General of each state, from state legislators, from the education committee of either or both houses, from the superintendent of schools and/or from local school boards. The regulations in effect for each particular school should be available in writing.

At the local level the lists of infractions for which a child may be spanked can be reduced. Hitting a child because of misspelled words or other academic errors has very few partisans any more and it should be comparatively easy to insist upon abolition. If swats are casual, irregular, unequally administered so that the Mayor's son gets away with murder, as it were, while the welfare child never escapes, it will be wise to insist on a written code made available to every student and every parent. Infractions and penalties should be spelled out in detail. When the list is too long and included too many trivialities, putting it in writing often has a shrinking effect because of possible embarrassment.

If these hurdles have been accomplished, the next step is to suggest an argue for parental approval. Educators generally give lip service to parent involvement and they have difficulty asking parents to help with phonics drills and rote math practice but shut them out of the disciplinary problems. Teachers are quick to blame parents for neglecting to teach good behavior to their children or to discipline them at home, yet loathe to confer about or if to paddle. To insist on this without the backing of law takes strong, determined parents and children completely convinced of their parents' values. Some parents have tried teaching their children civil disobedience. If they are ever in a situation where they are expected to accept blows, the children were instructed to say, "I am sorry, sir, but I an not permitted to bend over, My parents have forbidden. May I request, sir, permission to use the telephone?" Children capable of handling themselves well under such circumstances would rarely need to be so tested.

At the state level, legislative strategy depends upon present laws. If school board and site administrators are forbidden to stop any teacher from hitting at his or her discretion - as in Ohio - the first effort might be to try for local option. If the State of Ohio would relax a bit and permit each school board to compile its own disciplinary code, most might continue present free wheeling knock-about, but some would experiment with better ways and that often proves to be infectious because vandalism costs go down, scholarship goes up and community complaints are generally constructive.

If there is local option as in New York where over half of the districts have abolished all forms of corporal punishment, the effort to put the whole state in the honors column along with Massachusetts, New Jersey, Hawaii and Maine becomes possible. There a determined effort spearheaded by the Parent Teachers Association and aided by several strong young advocacy groups, the new York Civil Liberties Union, the Quakers Conflict Resolution Project, good publicity on television, support from the Board of Regents and many, many hardworking individuals for two years, came to nothing. The bill was introduced, passed the lower house, but was held in committee by a single stubborn man who refused to report it out so that the State Senate could vote on it. They will try again and they will probably win in the end. Angry individuals and enthusiastic reformers had best be warned however, by the experience of New York State that the logic and the humanity of protecting children from institutionalized abuse is not always enough to overcome the leaden lethargy that most Legislators exhibit in regard to powerless constituents.

In other states, other situations will require other strategies. The California parental approval law has reduced the amount and severity of physical punishment close to the vanishing point. Almost half of the school districts found the regulations so bothersome that it seemed easier to adopt for all the non-punitive methods of the majority of teachers. The law requires that in those districts where corporal punishment is to be used, every parent must be sent, each September, a note asking for signed permission to paddle, if deemed necessary, that particular child. Now it just so happens that the majority who are in favor of paddles, are in favor of them for other people's children. For their own, most people prefer to be in charge of whatever punishments are dished out. The percentage of parents who sign and return the slips giving approval (not merely permission) is not known, but sample surveys indicate it is far less than half and leaves the principal with the dilemma of what to do with two boys fighting when one set of parents have signed their approval and the other have not.

The custom of beating on the bodies of immature children will gradually diminish and the laws will follow custom. The important thing for American mothers and fathers is to recognize that ours is a government of the people, by the people and for the people and that they do not have to offer up their children on the sacrificial altar of inept educators. Regulations can be changed and they, with their friends

119

and neighbors, can do it. The time has long since passed when frightened ninnies need sit shivering at the kitchen table telling themselves, "I better not complain. They might pick on my baby still more."

Consultation on legal matters and legislative strategies may be secured from:

END VIOLENCE AGAINST THE NEXT GENERATION
977 Keeler Avenue
Berkeley, California 94708
PHONE: (415) 527-0454

or from the:

NATIONAL CENTER FOR THE STUDY OF CORPORAL PUNISHMENT AND ALTERNATIVES IN SCHOOL
#833 Ritter Hall South
Temple University
Philadelphia, Pennsylvania 19122
PHONE: (215) 787-6091

Legal Aid offices are available to those below the poverty line and some affiliates of the American Civil Liberties Union are ready, able and willing to offer their services.

CHAPTER ELEVEN

A GENERAL THEORY OF MOTIVATION

What makes Johnny run?

How do we persuade people to get going?

Advertisers think repetition does it. Or promises of increased attractiveness and popularity. Military men in conventional battle knew that a stirring drum roll and a macho image of the "outfit" could inspire men to superhuman deeds of valor and patriotism, even to laying down their lives. Educators search endlessly for the ultimate motivation that will mold children into quiet, obedient, courteous, diligent, neat, orderly, bright-eyed images of their idealized self.

This book has presented the case against pain and fear of it as motivator. We have also presented an array of alternatives. Which of these is best? Are some suitable for some children some of the time and others better for other children on other occasions? How do we choose for each child under what circumstances? Are there developmental stages? Are there social class differences? If so, how does it happen that some poor children escape into the professions and middle class or better? Is it possible that the destiny of a child is determined by the kind of motivators directed at him during the formative years? And what might determine which children from poor families are marked to be beaten as their parents were and which raised gently to be gentlemen?

An interesting explanation of these differences and the apparent exceptions to the general rule that parents raise children as they themselves were raised, may be found in the work of Murray Strauss in his studies of violence in the family:

> The linkage theory hypothesizes that socialization practices will tend to be congruent with the type of personality needed to cope with the typical life circumstances which the child will face as an adult... To the extent that use of physical punishment produces a child who is relatively high in overt aggression and low in

121

internatized moral standards and self direction, and to the extent that these traits are characteristic of working class communities, it can be said that the use of physical punishment is an appropriate pattern of socialization for working class children.

Obviously, however, such a pattern is dysfunctional for working class children who will be upwardly mobile... Working class parents who anticipate social mobility for their child...tend to adopt the socialization patterns characteristic of the class to which they aspire for their children.

John Kenneth Galbraith, in analyzing The New Industrial State, identifies the four levels of motivation as: compulsion, pecuniary motivation, identification and adaptation. Compulsion and pecuniary reward are obvious: the slave worked to avoid the lash, the wage earner works for money. Identification Galbraith describes thus: "The individual, on becoming associated with the group, may conclude that its goals are superior to his own." Even a ditch digger could be so motivated if the ditch drains a malarial swamp and the digger will benefit by the improved environment; he will then identify his values with those of his employers an work with a will. This goodwill cannot be purchased even though the digger was hired and is paid. The identification with the goals of the enterprise is an extra that adds to his diligence and output. The fourth motivation, adaptation, is still further removed from compulsion. The person goes along with a group enterprise, not so much because he believes in what they are doing, although he may do that also, but because he hopes to be able to get control and influence the direction of the effort according to his own plans. A politician, for example, works hard for the success of his party, not because he is always in 100% agreement, but because he thinks he can advance his own causes by being a good soldier and eventually rising to a position of command.

It will be worthwhile to follow Galbraith's thinking a little further for the light it may shed on the historical origin and the present effects of these various forms of motivation.

Compulsion and pecuniary compensation usually exist together. "The slave got the whip when he did not work; he got food and shelter of a sort when he did." The working man is rewarded with a paycheck but the fear of unemployment should he slack off acts as a compulsive force to keep him working as his employer directs. Both are motivated by fear of punishment and by hope of reward, although obviously the worker whose punishment is not physical has more pride and to some extent more choice. Punishment cannot exist in a pure form since the cessation of punishment is experienced as a reward. (The carpenter hits his thumb with the hammer because it feels good when he stops.) One might also argue that the reward of money or other materials does not exist in pure form either since the withholding of the reward is experienced as deprivation, a potent punishment. But the cessation of punishment and withholding of reward are weak motivators, merely the other side of the coin of the positive drives. It is also clear that compulsion, especially physical punishment, is the more elementary form. The Cheops was built with slave labor driven by the lash, and some evidence indicates that it took a major convulsion of thought for the Pharoah to hit upon the idea that if the slaves were doled a ration of grain at intervals, they might last longer. Pecuniary compulsion on the other hand drew farther and farther away from brute compulsion. Debate about the relative advantages enjoyed by American slaves in the agrarian South and the "wage slaves" in the industrial North raged in Congress in the 1850's but runaways were all in one direction even though the hours of labor were about the same and the pace in the North probably faster. There is no question but that pecuniary rewards will be chosen over compulsion even if the resulting standard of living is not conspicuously different. The position of women in the two economies is also markedly different though Galbraith does not consider this factor. The freedom from consort duty with the master is no inconsiderable boon; freedom from the need to labor during the child bearing years and the freedom to devote one's self to the care and rearing of children of one's on with a dependable wage earner as support, although not universal, was the common pattern and bespoke a greater pride and a greater degree of self determination among the families of wage earners. And, as we shall see, wage earning is compatible with high and more sophisticated forms of motivation while compulsion is not.

Identification and adaptation, Galbraith's terms for the higher forms of motivation may also be called intrinsic enjoyment and the grasp for power. Or they can be termed, espirit de corpse and command. Or perhaps the spirit of good workmanship and authority. These cannot be bought with money although they are not incompatible with it. But compulsion makes identification impossible. The broad rule holds, says Galbraith: "What is compelled cannot be a matter of

123

choice. Alienation, not identification, will be the normal result." "The serf, slave or prison occupant takes the goals of the organization with which he is associated as given and, eccentric cases apart, is alienated from them all. He does only what avoids punishment." As workmen's security has risen with the ability to find other jobs, unemployment compensation and welfare, the element of compulsion has lessened. Slavery has disappeared. With the drop in the amount of compulsion, the beginnings of identification can be combined with wage payments. But so long as compulsion is prominent the stage is set for disagreeable behavior by both the compelled and those who force them.

Beyond a certain point, money reward begins to lose its motivating power. A highly paid corporation executive does not work harder if his salary is increased from say $100,000 a year to $150,000 a year. It is assumed that he was giving his best for the lower figure. Indeed he would be insulted if anyone thought that the money was more important to him than the good of the company. Not only could he get a comparable return in another corporation quite easily, but his investments and savings could carry him for a long time should he prefer to look about or take an extended vacation. He is motivated because he has identified his goals with those of the company and works because he enjoys having "his" company prosper. There is pride in being able to say, "I'm with Standard Instruments." He may also hope to become a vice-president someday and influence the company to expand and diversify into a number of fields that he thinks are important and that interest him personally.

One last point from Galbraith before we return to schools. Power, he explains, was once associated with land and compulsion was the mode. When power passed to capital and the factory system, pecuniary motivation came to the fore. Lastly, "Identification and adaptation are associated with the technostructure." When the great land owners held serfs, they compelled their labor with physical violence. But slaves worked poorly in factories; wages were more productive of consistent effort. Now that the highly skilled technicians hold the power in large corporations, neither compulsion nor salary are the prime movers. Identification of personal goals with the organization and adaptation of the organization for the personal power it provides are the primary motivations.

When children in school these four modes are easily identifiable, but it is strange how a return to ancient ways, compulsion and a token economy are touted as new and scientific. Actually, they are seriously regressive and a return to the ideology of slavery. It is not a coincidence that reliance on punishment is greatest in rural schools and among schoolmen not more than one generation removed from the land. As as alternative to corporal punishment, a token economy, that is, little rewards (toy money), "excellent" stamps, smiling face chips or a blackboard tally are the same step forward that wages for employment were over slavery.

A mother of a retarded child told both the teacher and the bus driver to be firm with her child and even offered to provide them a stick to beat him into submission. Both declined. The bus driver in this instance was readier to move into the industrial age than was the teacher. She kept a pouchful of pennies and promised the boy one each day when he sat still in his seat for the whole trip. At the end of the week, he had five whole pennies in his pocket. He was no longer a slave, but a freemason, an employed artisan in sitting still and as such his morale rose and although he was not yet ready to sit still because he enjoyed the ride (step 3) or because he looked forward to getting successfully to school (step 4), he was on his way. The teacher unfortunately was stuck with a broken record about rewards being. "That's bribery!" she said disdainfully, but failed to identify her monthly paycheck as equally bribery. "There is a unique sanctity about what has been long believed," says the quotable Mr. Galbraith.

The third step with children is their acceptance of school and lessons as the normal, the right, the only game in town. They are not rebellious nor do they have to be bribed. Good grades are as satisfactory as the $100,000 salary of the corporation executive or the research department scientist; they do the best they can in any case. These children are not motivated by fear of punishment; by and large they are seldom physically punished at home anymore than their industrial counterpart is driven to the board room or lab with a cat-o-nine-tails. They make mistakes; they have off days, just as their fathers do but they are oftenest treated with patience and understanding, or at most raised eyebrows and an explanation of what is expected. If they play hookey occasionally, this is disapproved of about as much as is the vice-president's afternoon playing golf. In any corporation there is the counterpart of the slow learner who is carried along by the sheer mass of enterprise. His secretary may gripe, whose who work nearest him snicker and shrug, but by and large he does not retard the enterprise as a whole to any appreciable extent. In

125

any case, he is not physically punished. he may be demoted or given makework, but he will not be forced out into the cold especially if he is related to the president of the board. Slow and even difficult children could similarly be carried along by the educational enterprise without damage to the school, the other children or the teacher's sense of fitness. Indeed, they often are if they are related to someone in power in their particular community. The phenomenon is well known to small town teachers. The mayor's son gets away with murder; the doctor's daughter is forgiven and promoted regardless of her actual accomplishment.

Two eighth grade boys were caught glue sniffing by the shop teacher. Both were reported to the principal. One was threatened with the loss of his position as class president if he ever did it again; the other was sent forthwith to juvenile hall and tagged delinquent. Usually this kind of preferential treatment is laid to class differences and while this is certainly true, it does not lay clear the bare bones of the reason for the differential treatment. It is not only prejudice against lower class people; it also reflects the expectation of the respective parents. The class president's father was accustomed to the executive role and the easy overlooking of personal pecadillos. He treated his son as the president of the firm treated him: a confidential chat about the disadvantages of being suckered in on a bad deal. The delinquent's father was a marginal worker accustomed to being fired for drunken sprees and the punishment of unemployment. He handled his son harshly and "fired" him to the police. Those who see only heredity in this story have already forgotten that the fault in both boys was identical: glue sniffing in the woodshop. Fairness requires that the punishment fit the crime, that both boys be treated the same. They were. They were turned over to their fathers. Each father loved and had high hopes for his son; both were disappointed about the episode. The manner of handling it came out of each father's personal experience and the mode of motivation each had experienced. The fact that one boy finished college while the other seethed in jail was determined at the parting of the ways in eighth grade over a glue pot. "Class differences" neither explain nor excuse what happened. Lack of awareness was to blame. Lack of awareness that punishment escalates the chances of more difficulties, more rebellion, more retaliation, more lashing out at any handy target by the one who has suffered punishment.

The fourth step, that of going along in the hope

that one will be able to us the organization to one's own ends in good time, the politician type, can be seen in the student who does enough homework to get grades high enough to make the team. He goes along with school values for what he can get out of it that he likes by way of prestige. The student who does extra book reports to impress his English teacher so that he has a chance to make yearbook editor is functioning in the adaptation mode. This cannot be forced or bribed. A shy girl toyed with the idea of running for class secretary. Her mother was delighted and promised her a typewriter if she got elected. Suddenly, the joy went out of it. Either because it would then be her mother's victory and not her own or because of some conflict between mother and daughter the girl turned down the opportunity and refused to be a candidate. Rewards that work for the slave and the employed earner do not work with those motivated by levels 3 and 4 rewards.

Experiments at Stanford University[1] showed that nursery school children who played happily with a special set of paints and made many interesting works of art with them, lost all interest when they were offered reward for such work. Turning play into work was accomplished simply by offering to pay for it. The work went on as long as the rewards lasted, but the spontaneous interest that had been shown in the beginning evaporated. Rewards dropped the activity from that of an artist/executive to that of a menial wage slave and the attitude changed from, "Hey! Look what I made, Mom!" to "Do I HAFF ta?"

Thus, debates about punishments, rewards, grades, prizes, scholarships, as competing modes of motivating students proves not one is better than another but rather that they are graduations and are utilized depending upon assumptions regarding the child and expectations[2] of his occupation when grown. The sequence is not linear in the sense that the child starts at mode 1 and progresses to mode 4. Rather the child starts at mode 3, intrinsic interest, identifying with the activity as an end in itself. Experimenting just to find out, just to see what happens, just to see if he can, is the basis of the infant's activities until it is by verboten's on the one hand and requirements on the other. If the child's intrinsic motivation has been distorted, we must dip below the line to rewards or still lower for punishments. With this we would have to accept alienation, grudging obedience, and, unless intrinsic interest takes over, a minimal performance that will be abandoned as soon as the artificial motivational force stops or is out of

127

sight.

MOTIVATION

	REWARD	PUNISHMENT	MOOD
Slave or prisoner	Food and shelter	Whipping, shackles, solitary	Alienation
Wage earner	Paycheck	Fired	Obedience
Executive or skilled technician	Salary and interesting work	Sent to "boondocks"	Loyalty
Entrepreneur	Profits, power, acclaim	Acceptance of resignation, loss of prestige	Creative excitement

after J. K. Galbraith;
The New Industrial State

EDUCATIONAL MOTIVATIONS

	REWARD	PUNISHMENT	MOOD
"Predelinquent"	Recess, lunch etc. with others	Swat; cracks "Time out"	Alienation
Just kids	Tokens	Detensions Suspension	Obedience
Students	Good grades, interesting assignments	Poor grades, "counseling"	Loyalty
Youth leadership	Honors, scholarships extra responsibilities,	Loss of honors	Creative excitement

Teachers' motivations generally fall between categories 2 and 3 depending upon how they see themselves. If they are working primarily for a paycheck, they will put in just enough effort or apple polishing to keep from losing tenure. They will appear to obey the letter of the instruction handed them from the district superintendent or the Board of Education or whatever authority makes itself felt most conspicuously. Beyond that very little. Just as they themselves work in the obedience mood, they expect their students to accord them obedience. Their assignments and class lessons are likely to be dull and tied to the text. The students are bored sensing the lack of enthusiasm. There being no spark on intellectual curiosity the students do not catch fire and the lively among them are likely to try to inject some drama into the proceedings. This requires some extra effort to handle and the easiest, most natural way is to scold. From scolding it is but one easy step to the last resort.

It is safe to say that most teachers operated a step above that minimal level. It it were not so, schools would actually be in the conditions that the doomsayers shout that they are - totally decayed, depraved, dying, exploding, drying up, or whatever colorful adjective ingenuity can devise to shock. These exposés are extrapolated from rotten spots where a concentration of wage earner type teachers have congregated in communities where poverty, cultural transplantation or other factos have built up a neglected or needy student body. There is a certain amount of spread of the infection from these cancerous disasters, but the educational establishment as a whole is not on the verge of expiring.

Most, or at least many teachers, operate as level 3 executives or skilled techincians, for whom a good salary is essential, but whose expertise is far more than fulfilling minimum requirements. In contrast to the wage-bound teacher, they enjoy the work, the children, the challenge and do not consider themselves corny for their loyalty to the educational establishment. Not that they are always in agreement with it, but that they find ways to create a wholesome well organized, learning climate with a minimum of disciplinary problems. This group joins the teachers' organization, takes summer courses and criticizes stuffy regulations and excessive paperwork, not because this makes more work for themselves personally, while they would not mind, but because it hampers real teaching, wasting time away from the children and from the subject matter that is dear to their hearts. They are inclined to resent an incompetent administrator and ignore a good one since they do not need leaders to motivate them. An intrinsic fascination with the process of teaching is meat and drink to them and all they ask of the administration is to get the books there on time, do the dickering with the maintenance staff and interrupt as little as humanly possible. These teachers are best chosen, hired and let alone. Like their counterparts in the industrial world - the branch manager, for example, or the research staff -

they produce most when allowed a large share of autonomy.

Having identified with the educational establishment in the broader sense, (not necessarily with the local representative whom they may or may not respect) these skilled executive teachers are unlikely to teach controversial doctrines although they are sometimes accused of it, especially the social studies sector where doctrine that is old hat on the college campus seems far out and revolutionary to a rural board of education. The necessity for a history teacher to present communism, for example, as a form of government that requires understanding so that we as a democracy may deal with other countries that have chosen this type is not misunderstood at the university level, but it can and does raise a furor in places where time stands still and communism is still a godless evil lurking behind bushes to snatch their children away from them and their way of life. The new math, on the other hand, should have been considered controversial since there was no proof of its greater relevance and much indication that it leaves children without the ability to add up the grocery bill, balance a check book or figure out how much interest they are paying on a revolving charge account. But teachers went along with it. As a teacher of English explained when phonemes and morphemes were being introduced into fourth grade phonics, "Well, there it is. We'll see what we can do with it." Since they function in the loyalty mode themselves, they expect their students to similarly identify with educational goals and the roads thereto. In general, they get what they expect. If they are employed in a system in which corporal punishment is endemic, they answer surveys by agreeing that, yes, corporal punishment is sometimes necessary and they would not want to see it forbidden. They rarely, if ever, use it themselves or ask for the vice-principal to use it, but when they do need back-up and that is all the back up there is, they go along with it. Surveys of teacher attitudes, if not self serving rigs for confirmation of preferred positions, usually show that teachers prefer the status quo. That is: where it has been forbidden long enough to have become a tradition to "never lay a hand on a child" they are opposed to its return. Where it is in regular use they favor its retention. Educational innovation is unlikely to arise from this level of middle management, but neither are they effectively critical either of outmoded habit or of change for change sake. It would be better for schools if they were.

The true entrepreneur is unlikely to remain an

elementary or secondary teacher very long. He (most often a he) finished his doctorate, goes to law school or runs for public office. Driven more by ambition than I.Q., he uses his teaching experience as a stepping stone to trying his skills in a wider arena. Those who stay in education tend to move upward into positions of authority and become the best of administrators. Not to be counted in this category however, are those misfits who, scared witless by a roomful of children, in desperation accumulate the brownie points needed for an administrative credential, find a weak spot and move with a sigh of relief into the principal's office. These administrators in name only continue in the wage earner mode, didactic, uninspired and exacting implicit obedience from students and teachers alike. When these with their follow-the-manual mentality are in a position of authority over women (most often women) with greater intelligence and more concern for the students the school becomes a disaster area. The best teachers become devious or are driven out and the others identify with the punitive incompetent rather than with their original conception of the school as a haven of learning.

Women are often the victims of this double bind, perhaps because the traditional role of women has been to function on level 3, skilled technician, but to be rewarded on level 1 with bed and board as a slave or prisoner. Sometimes the punishments are also on this level, in which case of course, the mood became alienation rather than loyalty as expected. As professionals, women tend to trail these clouds of traditional subservience, and suppress any hint of ambition in the interests of their children, genetic or psychological. It is unfortunate. Under executive or entrepreneurial leadership, many teachers, both men and women, find it possible to enjoy a whiff of creative excitement by developing an original course of study tailored to the special contours of their own special group. Perhaps by taming youthful tyrants with a bold idiosyncratic grasp of the hurt in their hearts and a play-it-by-ear (third ear, that is) composition of symphonic variations on the standard curriculum they can weave harmony out of discordant jangles. The ability and the skill is there. Treated as executives, released from the bond of obedience (renamed "accountability") teachers could very well change the low road of educational deterioration with its thorns and ruts and stink of painful coercion onto the high road of responsible, creative, originality that can make of the task the also difficult, but enjoyable

131

business of jockeying high spirited students with
leadership potential into the winner's circle.

Children perform, not as we want, not as we
demand, not as we pray, but as we in our hearts expect
them to perform.

A CHARTER OF CHILDREN'S RIGHTS

All children born into this world shall be accorded a basic set of human rights. Among these are the right to a welcome, to health, safety, food, physical comfort, personal care, education, equal protection of the law, freedom to be a child, a gradually increasing autonomy, and respect as a person without regard to race, sex, or economic status of the parents.

1. **WELCOME** All children shall have the right to be wanted, planned for and welcomed by parents who expect to take responsibility for them to maturity.

> Legal implications: Universal availability of safe family planning services and supplies. Vigorous, funded research into no-fail methods without side effects, not limited to one sex and, if possible acceptable to all.
> Universal family life education including supervised experience with children of all ages.

2. **HEALTH** All children shall have the right to optimal health care during the prenatal period, during birth and all through childhood including attention to physical, dental, optical and other needs as well as psychological and other counseling and care. None shall be subjected to sedation or other behavior modifying medications for the convenience of caretakers.

> Legal implications: Massive funding for prenatal and child care for all; removal of legal bars to licensing of midwives, maternity centers, nurses in private practice, and well baby clinics separate from hospitals for the care of the diseased and wounded; sufficient staffing of institutions and community care homes so that drugs and restraints are minimal.

133

The right to treatment or to refuse treatment without consent of parents shall be assured.

3. **SAFETY** All children shall have the right to be protected against abuse whether physical, psychological or sexual, and against neglect, dangerous situations and brutalizing physical punishments at home and while under the care of others at school, recreational facilities and in other institutions temporary or permanent.

> Legal implications: Abolition of all corporal punishments whether or not deemed an educational procedure or for the correction of faults; strict enforcement of laws against unsafe toys, flammable clothing, lead based paints and other hazardous products; planning to eliminate dangerous crossings, unguarded pits, pools and other situational hazards and to provide safe play space within walking distance for all children. Accessible social services for abused, harshly punished or neglected children and their families, with prompt and permanent removal of children at serious risk.

4. **NUTRITION** All children shall have the right to be provided sufficient food of sufficient quality and variety to insure maximum health, growth and development of mental faculties. This shall include adequate nutrition during the prenatal period.

> Legal implications: Laws regulating adulteration, preservatives and additives of all kinds with the health of future generations taking precedence over profits and packaging convenience; elimination of "empty calorie" snack, candy and soft drinks from school cafeterias, and the provision of nutritious lunches for all school children.

5. **PHYSICAL COMFORT** All children shall have the right to clothing and housing appropriate to the climate of a quality to insure comfort and security.

> Legal implications: Condemnation of unfit housing units; enforcement of building codes that eliminate rats and vermin from all homes where children live;

support payments high enough to supply proper environment.

6. **CARE** All children shall have the right to enjoy a continuing relationship of trust with one primary and a few auxiliary adults who are involved in such relationship and who are not so overwhelmed with other responsibilities and activities that they cannot reciprocate. This right shall apply to children in institutions, in foster and adoptive homes as well as those with their natural parents.

> Legal implications: Establishment of psychological parenting as having legal parity with natural parentage. Neither are to be interrupted except if they prove dangerous to the child. The right of natural parents to claim their child shall not be extended indefinitely. The child placed in a foster or adoptive home shall be under the same regulations as a child in his natural home. Classifying a child as unadoptable because of parental rights and moving him from one set of caretakers to another shall cease.

7. **EDUCATION** All children shall have the right to full quality education, including physical, vocational and experiencial opportunities as well as an academic program without coercive threats, humiliations destructive of self-esteem, or the infliction of pain. Those for whom the standard curriculum and methods are ineffective shall have access to high quality alternative schooling. Racial, sexual and other stereotyping shall have no place in the text books, in the curriculum or determine participation in any activities. Religious education shall be at the discretion of the parents through puberty.

> Legal implications: Funding for education will need to take priority over other national needs.

8. **LABOR** All children shall have the right to play and work according to their maturity. They shall be free from excessive labor at home or elsewhere, but they shall have the opportunity to work at appropriate jobs that do not conflict with their education. They shall be paid a fair wage for work outside the home and encouraged to accept responsibility for a cooperative share of chores at home. Their earnings may not be confiscated by adults.

135

> Legal implications: Child labor laws need reassessment to protect those not now covered such as farm labor and to make more flexible the age of entry to the labor market under work/study programs, apprenticeships and other alternatives.

9. <u>LEGAL</u> <u>SERVICES</u> All children shall have the right to their own advocates in all legal matters including disputes over custody, adoption, inheritance and abuse. Those raised by other than their natural parents shall have access to information concerning their origin upon reaching majority.

Children shall be drawn into the juvenile justice system only for behavior proscribed for adults and only upon evidence admissible in adult cases and only after being afforded the same constitutional rights as adults. They may be incarcerated only upon clear and convincing evidence that they are dangerous to the safety of others.

> Legal implications: Complete revision of laws and customs giving natural parents rights over their children even though they refuse to parent them. Establishment of an interdisciplinary profession trained in both law and child development to act as child advocates.

10. <u>RESPECT</u> All children shall have the right to be respected as authentic, autonomous persons in all relationships. Medical, educational and psychological personnel working with children in the areas of service, teaching and research shall be meticulous in obtaining the child's as well as the parent's informed consent. Labelling with any possibility of becoming a self-fulfilling prophecy such as predelinquent or other pre- categories or "early manifestations of" shall be avoided except upon incontrovertible proof that is more than a statistical probability.

> Legal implications: Data banks must be monitored to insure access for correction by the subject to prevent misuse and erroneous input.

BIBLIOGRAPHY

Adams, Paul, M.D. Children's Rights. New York: Praeger, 1971.

Adler, Alfred. The Education of Children. Chicago: Gateway, 1970.

Alexander, F. and Ross H. The Impact of Freudian Psychiatry. Chicago: University of Chicago Press, 1961.

Anderson, John P. M.D. Research reported on Family Practice News. Sept. 15, 1974.

Ansbacher, Hans. The Individual Psychology of Alfred Adler. New York: Basic Books, 1956.

Anthony, E. J. "It Hurts Me More Than It Does You" - An Approach to Discipline as a Two Way Process. in Ekstein, R. and Motto, R. L. (Editors) From Learning for Love to Love of Learning. New York: Bruner Mazel.

Arendt, Hannah. On Violence. New York: Harcourt Brace Janovich, 1972.

Azrin, Nathan and Holtz, W. C. "Punishment." in Operant Behavior: Areas of Research and Applications. W. K. Honig, Ed. New York: Appleton-Century-Crofts, 1966.

Baer, Donald, PhD. "Let's Take Another Look at Punishment." Psychology Today, Oct. 1971.

Bagley, W. C. School Discipline. New York: Macmillan Co. 1923.

Bakan, David, PhD. Slaughter of the Innocents. San Francisco: Jossey-Bass, 1971.

Bakan, D. "The Effects of Corporal Punishment in School." Journal of the Ontario Association of Children's Aid Societies, Nov. 1971.

Bandura, Albert. Social Learning and Personality Development. New York: Holt Rinehard, Winston, 1967.

Bard, B. The Shocking Facts About Corporal Punishment in the Schools. Parents Magazine, Feb. 1973.

Barris, Wm. H., M.D. Statement made to Citizens Against Physical Punishment, Dallas, Tx. 1972.

Bayh, Birch. Opening statement, Hearings before the Subcommittee to Investigate Juvenile Delinquency

137

of the Committee on the Judiciary United States
Senate, Ninety-Fourth Congress: The Nature,
Extent, and Cost of Violence and Vandalism in Our
Nation's Schools, 1975.

Berne, Eric. Games People Play. New York: Grove
Press, 1964.

Blumenthal, M. et al. More About Justifying Violence.
Ann Arbor, Mi.: University of Michigan Institute
for Social Research, 1975.

Bible, The

Birmingham, S. The Grandees. New York: Harper Row,
1971.

Brady, E. D. (Quoted in) The Reform of Secondary
Education: A Report of the National Commission.
C. F. Kettering Foundation, 1975.

Brooks, H. M. Strange and Curious Punishments. Boston:
Ticknor, 1886.

Button, Alan. The Authentic Child. New York: Random
House, 1969.

Caffey, John, M.D. "Brain Damage from Whiplash Shaking
of Infants." in American Journal of Diseases of
Childhood, V. 124, Aug. 1972.

California State Advisory Committee to the U.S.
Comission of Civil Rights The Schools of
Guadalupe: A Legacy of Educational Oppression
April, 1973 (ERIC document ED 087583).

Castan, Frances. Alternatives to Corporal Punishment.
Scholastic Teacher, Sept. 1973.

Clark, Kenneth B. Introduction to: Corporal Punishment
and School Suspensions: A Case Study. Report of
the Citizens Commission to Investigate Corporal
Punishment in Junior High School 22. Mark
Monograph #2, Nov. 1974. New York: Metropolitan
Applied Research Center, 1974.

Cobb, Lyman. The Evil Tendencies of Corporal Punishment
as a Means of Moral Discipline in Families and
Schools, Examined and Discussed. New York: Mark
H. Newman & Co. 1847.

Cutts, Norma and Mosely N. Practical School Discipline
and Mental Hygeine. New York: Houghton Mifflin,
1941.

DeMause, L. History of Childhood. New York: Harper
Row, 1975.

Dreikurs, R. Psychology in the Classroom. New York:
Harpers, 1957.

Edelman, M. W. Children Out of School in America., A
report by the Children's Defense Fund of the
Washington Research Project, Inc.

Eggleston, Edward. The Hoosier Schoolmaster. New
York: Grosset and Dunlap, 1889.

Ernst, K. Games Students Play. Berkeley, Ca.

Celestial Arts, 1972.

Falk, Herbert. <u>Corporal</u> <u>Punishment</u>: A <u>Social</u> <u>Interpretation</u> <u>of</u> <u>its</u> <u>Theory</u> <u>and</u> <u>Practice</u> <u>in</u> <u>the</u> <u>Schools</u> <u>of</u> <u>the</u> United States. New York: Teachers College, Columbia University, 1941.

Fawcett, J. (Quoted in) Medical Progress has had little effect on an Ancient Childhood Syndrome, <u>Medical</u> <u>News.</u> J. American Medical Assn. 1972.

Freud, S. A Child is Being Beaten: A Contribution to the Study of the Origin of Sex Perversions. 1919. <u>Collected</u> <u>Papers.</u> V. 2, New York: Basic Books, 1959.

Galbraith, J. K. <u>The</u> <u>New</u> <u>Industrial</u> <u>State.</u> Boston: Houghton Mifflin, 1967.

Gibson, Ian. <u>The</u> <u>English</u> <u>Vice.,</u> London: Duckworth, 1978.

Gil, David. <u>Violence</u> <u>Against</u> <u>Children.</u> Cambridge, Ma.: Harvard University Press, 1970.

Glasser, Wm. M.D. <u>Schools</u> <u>Without</u> <u>Failure.</u> New York: Harper Row, 1969.

Glueck, Eleanor and Glueck, Sheldon. <u>Unravelling</u> <u>Juvenile</u> <u>Delinquency.</u> Cambridge, Ma.: Harvard University Press, 1950.

Goodwin, Frederick L. M.D. <u>Assessment</u> <u>of</u> <u>a</u> <u>School</u> <u>Punishing</u> <u>Instrument.</u> Berkeley, Ca.: The Last Resort, May/June, 1975.

Gordon, Thomas. <u>Effectiveness</u> <u>Training.</u> New York: Wyden, 1970.

Grealy, J. I. <u>Testimony</u> <u>for</u> <u>the</u> <u>U.S.</u> <u>Senate</u> <u>Committee</u> <u>on</u> <u>the</u> <u>Judiciary</u> <u>Subcommittee</u> <u>to</u> <u>Investigate</u> <u>Juvenile</u> <u>Delinquency,</u> April 16, 1975.

Grier, W. H. and Cobbs, P. M. <u>Black</u> <u>Rage.</u> New York: Basic Books, 1968.

Grossman, Moses, M.D. <u>Testimony</u> <u>in</u> <u>the</u> <u>case</u> <u>of</u> <u>Ortega</u> <u>v.</u> <u>Guadelupe</u> <u>Joint</u> <u>Union</u> <u>School</u> <u>District.</u> Santa Barbara Superior Court, 1973.

Hall, R. V. et al. The Effective Use of Punishment to Modify Behavior in the Classroom. <u>Educational</u> <u>Technology,</u> 1971.

Harris, J. <u>Testimony</u> <u>for</u> <u>the</u> <u>U.S.</u> <u>Senate</u> <u>Committee</u> <u>on</u> <u>the</u> <u>Judiciary</u> <u>Subcommittee</u> <u>to</u> <u>Investigate</u> <u>Juvenile</u> <u>Delinquency.</u> April 16, 1975.

Helfer, R. E. and Kempe, C. H. <u>The</u> <u>Battered</u> <u>Child.</u> University of Chicago Press, 1968.

Henry, W. <u>Spanking</u> <u>and</u> <u>Bondage.</u> Toronto: Consolidated Publishing Co. Time Books, 1970.

Hentoff, Nat. Corporal Punishment. in <u>Civil</u> <u>Liberties,</u> Nov. 1971.

Hentoff, N. Child Abuse in Schools. <u>Ladies</u> <u>Home</u> <u>Journal</u>, April, 1980.

Holt, John. <u>How</u> <u>Children</u> <u>Learn.</u> New York: Pitman,

1967.

Humphreys, Richard. Corporal Punishment: Reply to the Majority Report of Committee on Rules and Regulations of the Boston School Board Boston: Geo. H. Ellis, 1980.

Hyman, Irwin. Corporal Punishment in American Education. Philadelphia: Temple University Press, 1980.

Inequality in Education. Corporal Punishment. special issue Sept. 1978.

Jefferies, Doris. Considerations of the Social and Psychological Effects of Corporal Punishment on Children. Paper presented at the American Psychological Association Convention, Honolulu, 1972.

Johnson, J. M. Punishment of Human Behavior. American Psychologist. v. 27 p. 1033-1054, 1972.

Jones, Fredric. The Gentle Art of Classroom Discipline. in The National Elementary Principal., Sept. 1978.

Kozol, J. Death at an Early Age. Boston: Houghton Mifflin, 1967.

Ladd, E. T. "Moving to Positive Strategies for Order Keeping with Kids Accustomed to Restrictions, Threats and Punishments." Urban Education, 1972.

Lejeune, A. Review of Jennie, The American Mother of Winston Churchill. in Focus, San Francisco 1975.

Levy, G. Ghetto School. New York: Pegasus, 1969.

Mann, Horace. Life and Works, Boston: Lee and Shepard, 1891.

Maurer, A. Corporal Punishment. in The American Psychologist, Aug. 1974.

Maurer, A. The Last ? Resort. Ed. V. 1-9, Berkeley, Ca. End Violence Against the Next Generation. 1972 to date.

Maurer, A. Corporal Punishment Handbook. Berkeley: Generation Press, 1977.

McBeath, Marcia. Little Changes Mean a Lot. Englewood Cliffs, N.J.: Prentiss Hall, 1980.

Mercurio, J. A. Caning: Educational Rite and Tradition. Syracuse, N.Y.: Syracuse University Press, 1972.

Mills, Edna. Lifting Holy Hands. Christian Herald, Jan. 1971.

Moore, Kathryn M. "The Dilemma of Corporal Punishment at Harvard College." History of Education Quarterly, Fall, 1973.

Morris, D. The Naked Ape. New York: McGraw Hill, 1967.

Meyers, Bob. A Christian View of Corporal Punishment. in Saints Herald, Sept. 1973.

National Education Association. Task Force Report on Corporal Punishment, Washington, D.C.: N.E.A.

1972.

Newell, Peter. (Ed.) <u>A Last Resort?</u> Harmondsworth, Middlesex, England: Penguin Books, Ltd. 1972.

Orwell, George. <u>Collected Essays.</u> New York: Harcourt Brace, 1954.

Page, David. <u>Theory and Practice of Teaching or The Motives and Methods of Good Schoolkeeping.</u> New York: A.S. Barnes, 90th Ed. 1867.

Phi Delta Kappan. Editorial, Jan. 1973.

Radbill, S. "A History of Child Abuse and Infanticide." in <u>The Battared Child,</u> Helfer and Kempe, Eds. Chicago: University of Chicago Press, 1968.

Raichle, Donald. "The Abolition of Corporal Punishment in New Jersey Schools." <u>History of Childhood Quarterly</u> v. 2 #1, 1974.

Redl, F. and Wineman, D. <u>Controls From Within.</u> New York: Free Press of Glencoe, 1962.

Report of a Working Party on Corporal Punishment in Schools. <u>The British Psychological Society,</u> Leicester, England, 1980.

Richter, Derek, M.D. Article in <u>The Lancet,</u> Sept. 1974.

Rubel, Robert J. <u>The Unruly School.</u> Lexington, Ma.: Lexington Books, 1977.

Selye, Hans, M.D. <u>The Stress of Life.</u> New York: McGraw Hill, 1956.

Skinner, B. F. <u>The Behavior of Organisms.</u> New York: Appleton, 1938.

Skinner, B. F. Interview with Elizabeth Hall in <u>Psychology Today,</u> Nov. 1972.

Snyder, Ross, Snyder, Martha and Snyder, Ross Jr. <u>The Young Child as a Person.</u> New York: Human Sciences Press, 1980.

Spiegal, S. <u>The Last Trial; On the Legend and Lore of the Command to Abraham to Offer Isaac as a Sacrifice: The Akedah.</u> New York: Pantheon Books, 1967.

Stenhouse, L. <u>Discipline in Schools.</u> New York: Pergamon Press, 1967.

Strauss, M. "Some Social Antecedents of Physical Punishment: A Linkage Theory Interpretation." <u>Journal of Marriage and the Family</u> Nov. 1971.

<u>Times</u> (London) Educational Supplement, Oct. 27, 1974.

Tonningsen, E. "Three Swats with a Ten Ounce Paddle from Eighteen Inches Away - So It Goes." in <u>California School Psychology,</u> 1972.

Washington, K. <u>A Report on Conflict and Violence in California's High Schools.</u> California State Dept. of Education, 1973.

Welsh, R. S. "Severe Parental Punishment and Delinquency: A Developmental Theory." <u>Journal Clinical Child Psychology</u> Spring, 1976.

Wiggington, E. The Foxfire Book. Garden City, N.Y.:
    Anchor Doubleday, 1972.

Williams, G. and Money, J. Traumatic Abuse and Neglect
    of Children at Home. Baltimore, Md.: Johns
    Hopkins University Press, 1980.

Wolfgang, M. E., Figlio, R. & Sellin, T. Delinquency in
    a Birth Cohort. Chicago: University of Chicago
    Press, 1972.

Wyman, M. Progress in School Discipline. Remarks of
    Dr. Morrill Wyman of Cambridge, in support of the
    resolution to abolish the corporal punishment of
    girls in the public schools of the City, made in
    the Republican Caucus, Nov. 16, 1866. Cambridge,
    Ma.: James Cox, 1866.